Contemporary Studies in Literature

Eugene Ehrlich, *Columbia University*
Daniel Murphy, *City University of New York*
  Series Editors

Nathaniel Hawthorne

a collection of criticism edited by J. Donald Crowley

McGraw-Hill Book Company

New York • St. Louis • San Francisco • Auckland • Düsseldorf • Johannesburg
Kuala Lumpur • London • Mexico • Montreal • New Delhi • Panama • Paris
São Paulo • Singapore • Sydney • Tokyo • Toronto

123456789MUMU7987654

Library of Congress Cataloging in Publication Data

Crowley, Joseph Donald, comp.
  Nathaniel Hawthorne: a collection of criticism

  (Contemporary studies in literature)
  Bibliography: p.
  CONTENTS: Crowley, J.D. Introduction.—Martin, T.
The method of Hawthorne's tales.—Hoffman, D. Yankee
bumpkin and scapegoat king. [etc.]

  1. Hawthorne, Nathaniel, 1804-1864—Criticism and
interpretation—Addresses, essays, lectures. I. Title.
PS1888.C75   813'.3   74-22440
ISBN 0-07-014768-X

To my mother and to the memory of my father

Contents

Chronology

1804	Born July 4 in Salem, Massachusetts.
1808	Death of Hawthorne's father, a sea captain, in Dutch Guiana.
1813	Injury to foot limits Hawthorne's physical activity and promotes an interest in reading.
1819	Family returns to Salem after a year in Raymond, Maine; Hawthorne begins studies for college.
1821–25	Attends Bowdoin College with Longfellow and Franklin Pierce; graduates eighteenth in a class of thirty-five.
1825	Returns to his mother's home in Salem; instead of entering his uncle's business, lives for the next twelve years in relative seclusion, devoting himself to his writing.
1828	Publishes his first novel, *Fanshawe: A Tale,* anonymously and at his own expense, and then completely dissociates himself from the book.
1830–37	Publishes over forty tales and sketches anonymously or pseudonymously in newspapers, magazines, and annuals.
1836–37	Edits the *American Magazine of Useful and Entertaining Knowledge* and writes *Peter Parley's Universal History.*
1837	Publishes *Twice-Told Tales.*
1838	Becomes engaged to Sophia Peabody, a semi-invalid.
1839–40	Receiving a political appointment, takes up duties as Measurer in the Boston Custom House.
1841	Lives for about eight months in the Utopian community of Brook Farm, hoping to provide a home there for Sophia Peabody.

1842	Publishes an enlarged edition of *Twice-Told Tales* as well as *Biographical Stories;* on July 9 marries Sophia Peabody.
1842–45	Lives at the Old Manse, in Concord, comes to know Emerson and Thoreau; continues to write tales and sketches for magazines.
1846	Publishes *Mosses from an Old Manse*.
1846–49	Assumes duties as Surveyor in the Salem Custom House; writes very little.
1850	Publishes *The Scarlet Letter,* is immediately celebrated as America's leading literary genius, and enters his most productive years; moves to Lenox, where he and Melville become friends.
1851	Publishes *The House of the Seven Gables, The Snow-Image, and Other Twice-Told Tales,* and *True Stories from History and Biography.* The last of three children—Una, Julian, and Rose—is born, and the family moves to West Newton.
1852	Publishes *The Blithedale Romance, A Wonder Book for Girls and Boys,* and the campaign biography of Pierce.
1853	Publishes *Tanglewood Tales for Girls and Boys;* receives from President Pierce appointment as U.S. Consul at Liverpool, where the family lives until 1857.
1857–59	Lives in Rome and Florence; returns to England.
1860	Publishes *The Marble Faun* (*Transformation* is the English title); attempts unsuccessfully to write others—*Dr. Grimshawe's Secret, The Ancestral Footstep, Septimius Felton,* and *The Dolliver Romance;* returns to the Wayside in Concord.
1863	Publishes *Our Old Home*.
1864	Dies on May 11 while on a tour of New Hampshire for his health; buried on May 23 in Sleepy Hollow, Concord.

J. Donald Crowley

Introduction

In 1879 the young Henry James, writing about *The Scarlet Letter* almost thirty years after its publication, in effect summarized previous evaluations and anticipated accurately the critical opinion of future generations: "Something might at last be sent to Europe as exquisite as anything that had been received, and the best of it was that the thing was absolutely American; it belonged to the soil, to the air; it came out of the very heart of New England." Of all the writers associated with American romanticism, it is Nathaniel Hawthorne whose reputation down through the decades has been steadiest, whose stature has been most constant. Ever since 1850 he has held a high place in American literary history and has been considered one of the chief architects of the ways in which we interpret ourselves and our culture. Unlike Irving, Cooper, and Longfellow and the other Fireside Poets, Hawthorne did not enjoy an immediate popular and commercial success only to be regarded by most later critics as a writer of the second or third rank. He never suffered, as Poe and Whitman did, from scurrilous attacks on his personal character; nor—though he wrote several juvenile collections—has he ever, like Poe, at times been consigned in large part to the children's shelf of the library or to the titillating kitsch of the horror movie. Whereas *The Scarlet Letter* brought Hawthorne enduring acclaim, his good friend Melville's *Moby-Dick* marked for him the beginning of almost three-quarters of a century of critical neglect. The winds of intellectual fashion have buffeted both Emerson and Thoreau: for the generations of Americans who witnessed the spectacle of world wars and the Great Depression, Emersonian optimism seemed betrayed and irrelevant. But even in the period between the Civil War and World War I—when realism had gained its ascendancy—and, after it—when the naturalistic novel came and went—interest in and respect for Hawthorne and his romances remained vigorous. And his dark, brooding vision of

1

human experience has continued in the twentieth century to answer to our sense of many of the basic shapes of reality. Both the Gilded Age and the post-Freudian modern world, albeit for strikingly different reasons, have found Hawthorne's fiction worthy of passionate attention. In recent years all the prevailing modes of literary analysis and interpretation—historicist, philosophical, psychological, psychoanalytic, sociological, theoretical, and myth criticism—have discovered Hawthorne's imagination a still-rich lode to mine.

Although Hawthorne has never suffered full-scale assaults by detractors, there has been, amid all the praise, a fairly steady undercurrent of condescension and dissatisfaction in our response to his achievement. The world has had something of a lover's quarrel with Hawthorne. Emerson, for example, thought him to be a greater man than any of his books demonstrated; and Poe, after hailing his power of "originality," later judged his fiction to be merely "peculiar" because of its allegorical tendencies. Orestes Brownson saw him as "fitted to stand at the head of American Literature" but remarked that his first collection of tales, "excellent as they are, are not precisely what he owes to his country." Reviewing *Mosses from an Old Manse,* Melville compared Hawthorne to Shakespeare, and his admiration also led him to dedicate *Moby-Dick* to Hawthorne. Several years later, however, his praises, though again bold, are qualified: "Still there is something lacking—a good deal lacking—to the plump sphericity of the man. What is that?—He doesn't patronize the butcher—he needs roast-beef, done rare.—Nevertheless, for one, I regard Hawthorne (in his books) as evincing a quality of genius, immensely loftier, & more profound, too, than any other American has shown hitherto in the printed form." Although Twain admired Hawthorne too much as a superb American "stylist" to parody his "literary offenses" as he did Cooper's, he confessed to William Dean Howells that Hawthorne (and George Eliot) "just tire me to death." James himself, especially at the beginning of his career, although gratefully cognizant that Hawthorne had provided him with a genuinely American literary tradition, was inclined to reject that tradition as too "provincial," so eager was he to engage the denser European scene. Various early twentieth-century critics complained of what they took to be Hawthorne's lack of passion and insufficient social and political awareness. And in the last decade several voices have raised the lament that once one has done with *The Scarlet Letter* and perhaps eight or so classic tales, Hawthorne's works seem scarcely worth serious study. The other romances, tales, sketches, and notebooks, they say, are highly valued only because of our misguided piety.

This strange blend of intense but patronizing admiration marks our reception of Hawthorne as it does that of no other major American writer. Of the many sources of our ambivalence, the original one, curiously, is Hawthorne himself as his own critic. Throughout his career his letters and prefaces—even the fiction itself—are dotted with self-deprecating, self-parodying statements. He was given to view his tales as having "the pale tint of flowers that blossomed in too retired a shade," "sentiment" instead of "passion," "an effect of tameness" rather than "profundity." He could accuse himself of a lack of high seriousness and describe *Mosses from an Old Manse,* which included "Young Goodman Brown," "Roger Malvin's Burial," and "The Artist of the Beautiful," as "trifles" which "afford no solid basis for a literary reputation." Having just finished *The Scarlet Letter,* he felt compelled to complain in "The Custom-House" that he had been unable to write a more meaningful work—a novel—about the materials offered by his contemporary world. With each romance he wrote came a resolution to make the next one different, truer to his perception of what he called "the Present, the Immediate, the Actual." Writing to his publisher four years before his death he could in effect reject the instinctive direction of his art:

> My own individual taste is for quite another class of works than those which I myself am able to write. If I were to meet with such books as mine, by another writer, I don't believe I should be able to get through them. Have you ever read the novels of Anthony Trollope? They precisely suit my taste; solid and substantial, written on the strength of beef and through the inspiration of ale, and just as real as if some giant had hewn a great lump out of the earth and put it under a glass case, with all its inhabitants going about their daily business, and not suspecting that they were made a show of.

And at the end of his career, when physical illness and imaginative exhaustion forced him to give up his painful and abortive efforts to complete another romance—about an American in search of his ancestral home in England—he spoke defeatedly of "a certain ideal shelf, where are reposited many other shadowy volumes of mine, more in number, and very much superior in quality, to those which I have succeeded in rendering actual."

By no means all of the works Hawthorne "rendered actual" can be called completely well-wrought urns. Some of his tales and sketches, in fact, we prefer that he had never written at all; and his remarks about a seldom-read story called "Mrs. Bullfrog"—"it was written as a mere experiment" and "did not come from any depth within me"—could be

said of a number of his creative efforts. *The House of the Seven Gables,*
The Blithedale Romance, and *The Marble Faun,* on the other hand,
although obviously ambitious attempts and not lacking for advocates,
are nowadays often viewed as somehow marred in either conception or
execution. But precisely the same admissions must be made about virtually all our writers except James and Faulkner. Melville, Twain, and
Fitzgerald, for example, must each, like Hawthorne, rest his case on a
single superb full-length work when confronted with quantitative standards of measurement. Of Emily Dickinson's approximately 1,800
poems, probably a hundred or so rank as her greatest; and Whitman's
finest poetry comprises a similarly modest proportion of *Leaves of*
Grass.

Yet current condescension about Hawthorne's achievement appears not so much to reflect an exclusive dissatisfaction with his partial
failures as to epitomize the state of much contemporary criticism. During the 1950s and 1960s the various modes of formalist analysis that
dominated our literary studies elucidated brilliantly the major aesthetic
patterns and "poetic" unities of Hawthorne's individual works, especially his best works. So completely was this task performed that virtually nothing seems left now to be said about the "formal" aspects of
Hawthorne's greatness as we conventionally conceive of them: there
has for some years been the feeling that, as one reviewer put it in 1965,
"We did not, honest to God, need eighteen new articles on Hawthorne." To the extent that his fiction can be analyzed and understood
as a series of purely "literary" texts—that is, as self-enclosed artistic
constructs having a unique, independent nature and participating in no
referential relation to reality—we have convinced ourselves, perhaps
unjustifiably, that we "know" Hawthorne. And, although we have yet
to reach a solid consensus about those literary meanings, we have
become impatient with ostensibly new readings that offer still
subtler—but often mechanical and uninspired—reinterpretations of this
text or that.

Knowing as much as we do, we are still far from knowing all. As
the number of recent studies attests (the 1972 *MLA Bibliography* lists
126 entries for Hawthorne, second among American writers only to the
number of essays on Faulkner), there is a Hawthorne "problem" that
compels our constant reengagement. The Hawthorne we have tended
recently to know best and admire most—"Our Hawthorne," as Lionel
Trilling calls him—is limited to the writer of a relatively small number
of fictions that appeal to our taste for autonomous and powerful imaginative visions of "man's dark odyssey in an alien world." Ours is
not the same Hawthorne Henry James knew: his Hawthorne of the
"deeper psychology" encompassed much more of the canon. Our

Hawthorne is still further from the one his contemporaries thought they knew. Nor is ours to be equated with the Hawthorne he himself perceived for all we can so far tell. What we have instead is another in a long line of unfinished portraits. As Howells commented long ago, "We are always finding new Hawthornes, but the illusion soon wears away, and then we perceive that . . . he had some peculiar difference from them."

Howells's remark points to what must be seen today as one of Hawthorne's central triumphs: even after all the spilled ink—after so much intense and discriminating analysis and interpretation—we still have not been able to possess him. He remains for us a largely unsolved riddle. Nowhere is this more evident than in the disjunction between our biographical and our critical assessments. His contemporaries saw the man himself as a figure of mystery, hauntingly withdrawn and etherealized, and his fiction as consisting oftentimes of pleasant and endearing, because (so they thought) ultimately harmless, fantasies. In contrast, we reconstructed him as a well-adjusted and even dully normal citizen at exactly the same time we were discovering his tales and romances to be full of deep ambiguities and tension-ridden conflicts. For us, it seems, his life has become an open book to just that extent to which his works have yielded up ironies on top of impenetrable ironies. Shifting the inscrutability from the life to the art, we still find ourselves confronting, and insisting on, inscrutability. And we are still unable to comprehend to our satisfaction, even with our psychoanalytic studies, how the man and his fiction constitute an organic whole.

There are in fact many Hawthornes, as there are many uses Hawthorne would have us make of his fiction. When our criticism—and especially, I suspect, that reflection of our criticism which characterizes our classroom teaching—emphasizes the complexity and excellence of a few separate texts, we tend to lose sight of equally valuable and astonishingly different Hawthornes. The Hawthorne we have used best—the self-disciplined and highly conscious artist in an energetic quest for form—has undeniable claims on our attention. So too, however, does the Hawthorne of the entire corpus—the creator of a body of literature, the total meaning of which is greater than that derived from the sum of its parts. This Hawthorne is one who, while dedicated to the formal unity of the single work, also pursued those larger ideals of form arising out of the ways in which the meanings of all his works interpenetrate. In his own quiet, self-effacing way, he experimented—often tentatively; often, one feels, in calm desperation—to discover not only the appropriate forms but the very materials, the basic subject matter, he was convinced Americans needed to have fictions about. It was his desire, as he had his persona state in "Fragments from the Journal of a

Solitary Man,'' to create a literature of "deep and varied meaning" which would remind his reader that "he is an American." His aim, clearly, in saying that it was his purpose "to open an intercourse with the world" was in some sense to extend his art beyond the limits of pristinely aesthetic values. This Hawthorne is one we can know, not so much by an astute manipulation of the meanings of individual stories as *products,* but by an involvement in all those vaguely defined forces —historical, social, psychological, philosophical, and cultural—the intersection of which comprises that *process* by which Hawthorne's art came to be for his time and for ours. Knowing this Hawthorne, we can have a different understanding of the nature and causes of his failures and an appreciation of their importance precisely as failures. If we can take as our precedent Melville's intuition that "failure is the true test of greatness," we can come to know again the Hawthorne Melville praised, the Hawthorne who prompted him to say, "the immediate products of a great mind are not so great as that undeveloped and sometimes undevelopable yet dimly-discernible greatness, to which those immediate products are but the infallible indices."

To know this Hawthorne we must put aside what Allen Tate has called the "angelic imagination" and heed more habitually the full burden of Hawthorne's historical situation. Too few students are made aware of the extraordinary difficulties Hawthorne faced in nineteenth-century America simply by declaring his vocation as an artist. Though other writers had similar struggles, Poe was accurate in describing Hawthorne as *"the* example, *par excellence,* in this country, of the privately admired and publicly unappreciated man of genius." Almost every aspect of Hawthorne's creativity was conditioned by his acute awareness that for over twenty years he had no sympathetic audience. He occupied, he said, "an unfortunate position between the Transcendentalists . . . and the great body of pen-and-ink men who address the intellect and sympathies of the multitude." Believing that a genuinely democratic literature, by its very nature, demanded a nonelitist audience, he too wished to address that multitude—but on his own terms rather than on those of what he called a "damned mob of scribbling women." We have as yet not taken the full measure of his achievement in the context of this condition. Faced with the necessity of creating an American audience as well as a genuinely American art, Hawthorne experimented energetically with ways to accommodate the needs of his readers to the requirements of a fiction he thought would be authentic for them. He was often led to begin with a literary convention or stereotype familiar to that audience and then to wrench the cliché—the worn-out form or situation or sentiment—so as to endow it with the force of his originality and thus to transform it into a fresh vision that answered to something deep in the character of the American psyche. His use of Gothic paraphernalia and the staples of the sentimental-historical imitations of Scott, so popular in his day, are but two examples of the sort of meretricious materials he was often able to reshape and give import. "The world, nowadays," he was convinced, "requires a more earnest purpose, a deeper moral, and a closer and homelier truth than [Scott] was qualified to supply it with." Another of his experiments lies in his much misunderstood treatment of his audience's penchant for the explicitly stated moral. Time and again in his fiction Hawthorne managed to invent strategies that would invite all his readers to free themselves from relying on the emotional comforts of such naïve didacticism while allowing those readers incapable of being so instructed to have their normal fare.

That is to say, there is something beautifully collaborative about Hawthorne's work; there is a noble humaneness in him and in his vision of the humanizing function of art that should be especially impressive to us who have become too accustomed to the crass and manipulative crudenesses of the mass media. Hawthorne was shrewd enough in the ways of pandering to the masses. But instead of exploiting his audience's limitations, he gave himself up to the task of elevating the taste and consciousness of his readers, even when plagued by the persistent doubt that he had many readers.

We have yet to account fully for the "affective" dimensions of Hawthorne's genius, the techniques he invented to compel Americans into an awareness of their very relationship with literature. We have not yet perceived, for example, the seriousness of motive behind his collections for children. He could speak of them at times as some of his "drudgery," and he made no secret of his hope that such volumes would be more profitable than his other tales; but he was plainly devoted to them as a means of enlarging, if not for his time at least for the future, the range of American literary sensibilities. Although he was, as his sister-in-law once described him, "a man talking to himself in a dark place," those collections are manifestations of his efforts to make fiction available to a hard-headed, pragmatic, antipoetic culture distrustful of or oblivious to the realities of imaginative experience.

Faced with such necessities, Hawthorne did not—indeed, could not—define the primary function of the imagination as the creation of self-contained symbols with the purpose of overwhelming his readers in order to make them forget the real world around them in the way that, say, Kafka's symbols do. As the distinctions his prefaces draw between the romance and the novel make clear, it was his peculiar task, instead, to take into account the real world while insisting on the uses of fantasy. Unlike Kafka, he had to build bridges between reality and the imagination. If we are ever to understand the largest sense of form operative in his work, we must be aware that his art invariably addresses the open, indeterminate spaces—the formless interstices—between the imagination on the one hand and the world of actuality on the other. What that dimension of form often derives from and even consists of is the quality of *voice* that quietly dominates as it deepens both materials and themes. It is a voice as rich as it is low-keyed; at once private and public, self-concealing and self-revealing, probing yet decorous, doubtful and assertive. It is, above all, a collaborative voice whose tones first invite the reader to aid in the imaginative process and then lead him gradually to explore the unfamiliar territory of the deeply ambiguous and problematic nature of experience in the New World. Because it is what Frost called "a still, small voice," we are inclined to miss many of its resonances. Whitman's voice, usually direct and explicit as well as expansive, is the one we normally think of as sounding an authentically new American note. But as different as Hawthorne's tone is from Whitman's, his is also, in its modulated nuances of hope and skepticism, a genuinely American voice: its registers contain an equally radical sound of freedom and have a capacity to evaluate even more sharply the disturbing consequences of that freedom.

In our fascination with Hawthorne as the moral historian of New England Puritanism—the Hawthorne who created the great tales that stress the inescapably guilt-ridden terms of human identity and New World history—we have probably underestimated the Hawthorne who might be called a social and cultural historian. The image of the house and the theme of psychic homelessness, for example, are persistent concerns throughout his work. They define his failures as well as his successes and are central to those larger issues and conflicts that organically bind all his works together. In his own life Hawthorne always desired to have his own home and always, once he had settled in anywhere, quickly became restless and eager to move on. "It is folly for mortal man to do anything more than pitch a tent," he once complained; and in his writing he tried compulsively and for the most part futilely to resolve these ambivalences. He attempted to sustain the idea of home as a symbol of permanence and stability—as a stay against the confusion of ceaseless change. At the same time, he was the first of our writers to give the house a special metaphorical status as the symbol of individual consciousness and thus of the freedom of the mind and the imagination. That is, he tried to make it stand simultaneously for form and security and for mobility, freedom, and progress. It is not surprising that he could never fully resolve the psychic tensions arising out of these diametrically opposed value systems. When we consider our own continuing ambivalence toward "home," however, we can appreciate the

depth of the contradictions Hawthorne was courageously confronting.
Even in the twentieth century, when Americans are still the only people
in the history of Western civilization to be a society of home owners,
there is something compulsive and uneasy in that phenomenon. For,
curiously, we have managed—with our government-subsidized ideals
of low-cost housing intended to stand for only a single generation and
our extravagant and grotesque efforts to redesign the house as a vehicle
capable of moving us through space and time—only to attenuate the
terms of that conflict. Our own difficulties tell us that Hawthorne is a
writer who dared to address levels of American consciousness and experience that defied, and still defy, abiding formal controls. To that
extent, we understand his failures only as we know them as our own,
our culture's; and so we understand that Hawthorne's was a powerfully
prophetic voice.

His art, then, has a compelling modernity. Alfred Kazin recently
wrote, "Twentieth-century American writers do not generally feel
much relation to Hawthorne. To those who value past writers because
they influence our living and thinking *now,* Hawthorne is unreal." Such
a judgment suggests that we have not come to know Hawthorne completely perhaps because we want to know him in a bluntly direct way.
But it is not simply by his works alone that we can know him. There is
that Hawthorne who lives on for us, in transmuted forms, in the fiction
and poetry of other writers. There is, for example, the Hawthorne Emily
Dickinson found "enticing, appalling," the source of "Further in
Summer than the Birds." And there is, of course, the Hawthorne whom
James came late in his career to realize had existed all along for him
—Hawthorne, the alienated symbolist who had generated in the ro-
mance form a sense of "the great complication" and discovered for
James the wherewithal of "the international theme," a sense of the
past, the heroic tensions between life and art, and a symbolism capable
of bearing the burden of the moral universe. There is the Hawthorne
Frost used in "The Wood-Pile," "Desert Places," and "Spring
Pools." While writers as different as Robert Lowell, Flannery
O'Connor, Jorge Luis Borges, and Robert Penn Warren have expressed
their direct indebtedness to Hawthorne, the nature of his largest influence transcends such explicit lines of descent. We fail to know him
when we fail to realize that, if much of our fiction is different from his,
it is different because his fiction helped make ours free to be that way.
His importance in the development of an American literary consciousness can safely be measured by differences as well as similarities.

The essays collected here are representative of recent critical efforts to define exactly the character of Hawthorne's achievement, the
nature and causes of his failures, the basic assumptions of his art, and

the conditions of his development. They reflect as well something of that range of controversial attitudes which show that we have yet to agree on how to take Hawthorne. Intended essentially as an introduction to the various ways we now see him, the essays also suggest some of the questions that will determine the direction of future Hawthorne studies.

Terence Martin

The Method of Hawthorne's Tales

Hawthorne's primary concern as a writer was to gain access to what he once called "the kingdom of possibilities." Repeatedly, he speaks of his need to attenuate the American insistence on actuality. The burden of the prefaces to his major romances is that he requires a latitude for his imagination, a "neutral ground" set metaphorically between the real world and the imaginary. His romances take form—he would have us believe—in the context of poetic precincts and fairy lands, part of the geography of the "neutral ground." Hawthorne's effort to dilate reality for the purposes of his art ends only with the significant admission in his introductory letter to *Our Old Home* in 1863 that "the Present, the Immediate, the Actual, has proved too potent for me."

What all such statements signify is that Hawthorne needed a fiction to create fiction. And long before he turned his energies to the romance, he had confronted the problem of how to bring his fiction into being in the form of the tale. The method of Hawthorne's tales reveals the achievement of a writer who had to establish the *conditions* of his fiction in the very act of creating that fiction itself. As he himself acknowledged, Hawthorne did not improve steadily as a writer of tales. Some of his best work came surprisingly early: "My Kinsman, Major Molineux" was first published in 1831, "Young Goodman Brown" and "The May-Pole of Merry Mount," in 1835. Slight tales appeared in the same year with major tales. *Twice-Told Tales* (1837) was considered superior as a collection to *Mosses from an Old Manse* (1846) by Poe,

From Hawthorne Centenary Essays, *edited by Roy Harvey Pearce, and Copyright © 1964 by the Ohio State University Press. Revised by the author for publication here and reprinted by his permission and that of Ohio State University Press.*

Melville, and most later critics. Yet "Rappaccini's Daughter" (1844) and "Ethan Brand" (1851) clearly attempt and achieve more than do, say, "The White Old Maid" (1835) and "Mrs. Bullfrog" (1836). The movement of Hawthorne's tales, indirect and often unsure, is toward *The Scarlet Letter*. But it took twenty years of striving before Hawthorne's triumph in *The Scarlet Letter* exhausted the tale for him as a working form even as it transformed the tale into the romance.

THE CONDITIONS OF FICTION

Hawthorne opens "The Hollow of the Three Hills" (1830) with an abrupt evocation of a mysterious past: "In those strange old times, when fantastic dreams and madmen's reveries were realized among the actual circumstances of life, two persons met together at an appointed time and place." He begins, that is, by equating the real and the fantastic. If there were such a time, we see immediately, when dreams and reveries existed as a part of actual life, then surely there could be no more congenial setting for his tale. As the condition of his fiction, Hawthorne postulates the existence of "strange old times," then uses the immense latitude he thereby acquires to relate a tale of domestic tragedy from a thoroughly non-domestic point of view.

By means of the crone's powers, with their suggestion of Satanic darkness, the lady of the tale can look back into her life to see the tragic consequences of her actions. She has wrung the hearts of her parents, betrayed her husband, and "sinned against natural affection" by leaving her child to die. Amid a setting redolent of witchcraft and evil, she experiences her visions of society. After each vision, Hawthorne makes a transition back to the hollow, thereby reinforcing the reality principle of the tale. For this is where the lady's sins have led her. She must consort with witchcraft and deviltry if she is to have even a glimpse of society. To measure the distance of her fall, she must make use of powers antithetical to heart and home. Taking advantage of the latitude assumed in (and achieved by) his abrupt opening sentence, Hawthorne has turned the world as we ordinarily know it inside out—we see society only in momentary visions from the standpoint of the marvelous. He has managed the form of his tale so that it embodies in a unique way a theme characteristic of his work.

The opening sentence of "The Hollow of the Three Hills" constitutes a Hawthornesque variation of the time-honored opening of the fairy tale. It was a method of getting his fiction immediately under way which Hawthorne would use repeatedly. "The Great Carbuncle" (1836), for example, begins, "At nightfall, once in the olden time. . . ." In "The Lily's Quest" (1839), this has become "Two lovers, once upon a time. . . ." And in "Earth's Holocaust" (1844), "Once upon a time—but whether in the time past or the time to come is a matter of little or no moment. . . ." By adopting the convention of the fairy tale, Hawthorne achieves at a stroke the imaginative freedom he requires. And most often he shapes the ensuing tale into a fable complete with a moral regarding human wisdom or folly. The lesson of "Earth's Holocaust" is that reform will fail if the human heart is not first purified. "The Great Carbuncle" points up the wisdom of rejecting a jewel which would dim "all earthly things" in favor of the "cheerful glow" of the hearth. "The Lily's Quest" spells out laboriously the idea that happiness is predicated on eternity. Wrought with greater discipline, "The Hollow of the Three Hills" does not offer a moral refrain. What it says about human guilt and woe is implicit in the achieved drama of the tale, which stands as the best evidence of what Hawthorne could realize in fiction by adapting the method of the fairy tale to the uses of the imagination.

Any writer who faces the necessity of establishing the conditions of his fiction will feel a concomitant need to explain processes and intentions to his reader. And such a writer will pay a price for doing so much by himself; to succeed as an artist, he will have to do the work of generations in a single lifetime and incorporate the mistakes, false starts, and indirections that ordinarily dwarf careers into the broad investment of his genius. Hawthorne would probably have written fewer slight tales had he worked with the legacy of an older literature. Alternatively, he might well have achieved less; for there would simply have been less to do.

In keeping with Hawthorne's stated intention, "The Threefold Destiny" is subtitled "A Fairy Legend." And it is among a number of Hawthorne's tales having this kind of subtitle. "Fancy's Show Box" is "A Morality"; "David Swan" is "A Fantasy." Such subtitles are neither elaborations of the main title itself nor do they function as alternative titles in the manner of subtitles in many eighteenth- and early nineteenth-century novels. In "Night Sketches: Beneath an Umbrella" (1837) and in "Egotism; or, the Bosom Serpent" (1843), to take but two examples, Hawthorne did use subtitles in these conventional ways. But "A Morality" and "A Fantasy," as well as "A Parable" [for "The Minister's Black Veil" (1835)], "An Imaginary Retrospect" [for "The Village Uncle" (1834)], "An Apologue" [for both "The Man of Adamant" (1836) and "The Lily's Quest"], and "A Moralized

Legend" [for "Feathertop" (1852)]—such subtitles are attempts to describe the *form* of the tales. They tell not what the tale is about, but what the tale is. They are explicit indications of the *kind* of fiction Hawthorne is endeavoring to write.

Characteristically, Hawthorne uses twilight as an analogue of the "neutral ground" to achieve his imaginative effects. "The white sunshine of actual life," he says in "The Hall of Fantasy" (1843), is antagonistic to the imagination, which requires access to a region of shadow if it is to function creatively. Young Goodman Brown begins his shattering journey into the forest at sunset. "The Great Carbuncle" begins at nightfall. And the settings of "The White Old Maid," "The May-Pole of Merry Mount," and many other tales depend heavily on twilight, shadow, and Gothic effects.

Twilight is the middle time, between the noon of actuality and the midnight of dream. It corresponds to the point between yesterday and tomorrow that constitutes the setting of "The Haunted Mind" (1834), that profoundly metaphorical sketch in which Hawthorne presents a musing dramatization of the creative process. On the borders of sleep and wakefulness, dream and reality meet and merge. The actual and the imaginary each partake of the nature of the other; the conditions of fiction are displayed in paradigm. But just as it is difficult to remain on the borders of sleep and wakefulness, so the twilight atmosphere can be difficult to sustain. Before the legends themselves are told, the narrator of "Legends of the Province House" (1838-39) draws "strenuously" on his imagination in an effort to invest a contemporary tavern with an aura of the past. While concerns of historical grandeur and plebeian actuality remain with Hawthorne's narrator in the framework, the inner tales move expansively in a twilight of legend. At the end of a tale, the narrator strives to maintain the illusion it has created; but a spoon rattling in a tumbler of whisky punch, a schedule for the Brookline stage, and the *Boston Times*—couriers of "the Present, the Immediate, the Actual"—quickly defeat his efforts. "It is desperately hard work," he concludes, "to throw the spell of hoar antiquity over localities with which the living world, and the day that is passing over us, have aught to do."

In his legends of the province house, and in other tales as well, Hawthorne equates revolutionary tendencies with the democratic aspiration of the people; colonial history comes to prefigure the spirit of the American Revolution. Wearing old Puritan dress, the Gray Champion (1835) answers the cry of an oppressed people. Typically, as a figure evoked onto a historical neutral ground by the imagination, he stands between the colonists and the British soldiers in an "intervening space," with "almost a twilight shadow over it"; when he disappears some think he has melted "slowly into the hues of twilight." But he will be at Lexington in the next century, says Hawthorne, "in the twilight of an April morning." For the Gray Champion "is the type of New England's hereditary spirit," opposed equally to domestic tyranny and to the step of the invader.

Endicott's defiance of English authority in "Endicott and the Red Cross" (1836) is presented explicitly as a rehearsal for the American Revolution. Brooding over the meaning of American colonial history, Hawthorne's imagination came to see and to formulate a continuity in the American Revolutionary spirit. At a time when American writers labored under the constraints of a lack of tradition, Hawthorne employed the colonial past as one effective way of achieving the imaginative latitude he required. His sense of the past is not at all simplistic. If the Puritans embody a spirit that was to find fullest expression in the American Revolution, they are also, in Hawthorne's presentation, harsh, cruel, blind to all liberties but their own. Endicott can resist oppression in one breath and show himself a raging zealot in the next. "Let us thank God," Hawthorne writes of the Puritans in "Main Street" (1849), "for having given us such ancestors; and let each successive generation thank Him, not less fervently, for being one step further from them in the march of ages." In his tales of colonial times, Hawthorne makes Americans see what they had been as a way of showing them more fully what they are.

". . . WHAT PRISONERS WE ARE."

During the years immediately following his marriage in 1842, Hawthorne wrote a number of tales distinct in form from his previous work. In these tales—which include "The Procession of Life," "The Celestial Railroad," "The Christmas Banquet," "A Select Party," and "The Hall of Fantasy"—he examines subjects such as reform, social organization, human folly, and modern religiosity. "The Procession of Life" supplies a term to describe the group as a whole. They are, in one way or another, processionals. They are set perhaps in a vague banquet hall, on an undefined prairie, or in a castle in the air; they deal with assemblages of people who are characterized collectively. In his processionals, Hawthorne assumes such largeness of treatment that he necessarily confronts general human problems in a general way. No personal drama of guilt or suffering could be portrayed effectively by means of such a form, which explores subjects in themselves and achieves latitude by the expedient of perspective. Surely not among his best tales, the processionals do show Hawthorne striving for the kind of effect that only experimentation with the form of the tale would yield.

Among the subjects considered in the processionals is the role of the imagination in human life. "A Select Party," for example, describes an "entertainment" given by a man of fancy at "one of his castles in the air." Many on earth lack "imaginative faith" and are unworthy to attend. But among the admired guests are the Master Genius of the age, who will fulfil the literary destiny of his country, and Posterity, who advises all to live for their own age if they would gain lasting recognition. During the festivities, a sudden thunderstorm extinguishes the lights and reduces the party to confusion. "How, in the darkness that ensued," writes Hawthorne, the guests got back to earth, or whether they got "back at all, or are still wandering among clouds, mists, and puffs of tempestuous wind, bruised by the beams and rafters of the overthrown castle in their air, and deluded by all sorts of unrealities, are points that concern themselves much more than the writer or the public." He concludes with the admonition that "people should think of these matters before they thrust themselves on a pleasure party into the realm of Nowhere."

"A Select Party" teaches a complex lesson about the imagination. "Imaginative faith," as defined by Hawthorne, would seem to be a highly desirable trait; those who lack it are bound heavily to the earth. The presence of the Master Genius and of Posterity seems to add ballast to the more fanciful "creatures of imagination"—such as a cadaverous figure who is in the habit of dining with Duke Humphrey (that is, not eating at all). The tone of the piece is at once serious and sportive. Yet there is the final doubt that the party-goers can get back to earth. In a context of frivolity, Hawthorne's admonition comes as a joke. And it is indeed a joke—on the reader as well as the party-goers. We begin to laugh, then realize that the guests, bruised and misled, may be trapped in the realm of the imagination. But there is more to our realization; for in reading the tale, we, too, have been trapped, artistically sandbagged (for it is, after all, Hawthorne's party), forced to enact the foolishness of the party-goers and to share, in some surprise, their fate.

In "The Hall of Fantasy," Hawthorne ponders the "mystic region, which lies above, below, or beyond the actual." The Hall has its obvious dangers: some mistake it for "actual brick and mortar"; others live there permanently "and contract habits which unfit them for all the real employments of life." Still, for "all its dangerous influences, we have reason to thank God that there is such a place of refuge from the gloom and chillness of actual life." Those who never find their way into the

Hall possess "but half a life—the meaner and earthlier half." But the imagination has a final value, crucial and unambiguous. In "The New Adam and Eve" (1843), Hawthorne's thesis is that we have lost the means of distinguishing between the workings of nature and those of art. "It is only through the medium of the imagination," he goes on to say, "that we can lessen those iron fetters, which we call truth and reality, and make ourselves even partially sensible what prisoners we are." Implicit here, in its largest and most general manifestation, is the motif of withdrawal and return basic to Hawthorne's fiction. One withdraws into the realm of imagination, views the rigorous confinement of life, then returns to the world with a fuller understanding of the human condition. The ultimate function of the imagination is thus to serve as a unique and judicious critic of reality.

The role of fiction is the product of the role of the imagination. At their best, Hawthorne's tales—public proof that the author has returned from a private journey into the imagination—lessen the fetters of reality so that we may see "what prisoners we are." At their best, the tales invite us to consider the difficulties man faces because he cannot face his humanity. The tales tell us that man must acknowledge his dependence on (even as he should rejoice to participate in) "the magnetic chain of humanity." The alternative is abstraction, a preference for idea, which breeds pride, isolation, and ultimate self-destruction.

The cancer of obsession threatens any Hawthorne character —scientist, man of religion, artist—who prefers an idea to a human being. Aylmer and Rappaccini; Richard Digby (Hawthorne's "man of adamant"), the Shakers, and the Puritans and Quakers in "The Gentle Boy" (1831); the painter in "The Prophetic Pictures" (1836)—all seek to exist on the high, desolate plane of idea beyond the slopes of compassion and love. In historical tales, too, Hawthorne's concern for humanity is evident. The terms of his presentation change: tyranny and oppression represent abstraction, the insistence on idea; the will of the people—democracy—represents humanity. The Gray Champion, a people's hero, resists oppression, which Hawthorne defines as "the deformity of any government that does not grow out of the nature of things and the character of the people." For all his irritability and iron nature, Hawthorne's Endicott stands likewise for the people; thus, he can legitimately oppose any force which seeks to abrogate the rights of the colonists as human beings. And in "Edward Randolph's Portrait" (1838), Lieutenant Governor Hutchinson risks the terror of a "people's curse" by allowing British soldiers to occupy the fort.

If the oppressor seeks to abuse man in history, the reformer seeks to disabuse man of history; both dehumanize. To make mankind conform to the good as he sees it, the reformer wields his one idea like a flail. He repudiates history as the record of man's imperfection and seeks to destroy human foibles by the purity of his idea. The spirit of reform that spreads wildly in "Earth's Holocaust" seeks to burn away the follies and fripperies of the past. But all reformers overlook the nature of the heart (which is to say, the nature of man). Unless the heart is purified, says the dark stranger in the tale, "forth from it will reissue all the shapes of wrong and misery" which the reformers have burned to ashes.

In "Ethan Brand," Hawthorne articulates most explicitly the theme of a man of idea that had run through his fiction for almost twenty years. The definition and focus of the tale are precise; an obsession with one idea has completely vanquished the heart, turning it to marble. "Ethan Brand" bears the subtitle "A Chapter from an Abortive Romance," and there are several references in the narrative to episodes that have supposedly taken place at an earlier time. Hawthorne presents us with a conclusion, a final chapter. And incomplete as it may be with reference to his original conception, it has a ring of finality, the authority of a literary work that embodies a theme simply and precisely.

Ethan Brand commits a mighty sin of presumption which prefigures his final despair. The quest to commit a sin so vast that God cannot forgive it becomes itself the Unpardonable Sin. In the hour of his greatest despair, Ethan Brand stands revealed as a success; his quest becomes a parable of how to succeed at spiritual self-destruction. And his triumphant suicide is a final gesture for many a Hawthorne character who has destroyed his humanity over a period of years. The unlettered and earthy, however, are given an anti-climactic dividend in the tale. When Bartram finds the bones of Ethan Brand in the lime kiln, he decides that "it is burnt into what looks like special good lime; and, taking all the bones together, my kiln is half a bushel the richer for him." By half a bushel, the bones of Ethan Brand contribute to Bartram's well-being. By half a bushel, Ethan Brand serves the mundane purposes of a humanity he has scorned.

To repudiate humanity, in Hawthorne's fiction, is to fail spectacularly; to accept humanity is to succeed domestically. Throughout the tales, heart and hearth are intimately related. The bantering praise of the open hearth in "Fire Worship" (1843) has its serious counterpart in "The Vision of the Fountain" (1836), in which the fireside domesticates the vision. Ralph Cranston in "The Threefold Destiny" discovers that home is where one's destiny awaits. Dorothy Pearson, the bringer of love to the gentle boy, is like "a verse of fireside poetry." Both "The Great Carbuncle" and "The Great Stone Face" (1850) draw morals concerning the futility of searching abroad for values inherent in domesticity. Wakefield (1835) is an apostate from home; whimsy, stubbornness, and a creeping paralysis of will transform him into the "outcast of the Universe." The characters in "The Ambitious Guest" (1835), unsettled by the young man's contagious thirst for fame, are killed by a rockslide when they rush out of their house in search of shelter; their home stands untouched. Home, clearly, is of the heart. To be heartless is to be homeless.

The great importance of Sophia and a home in Hawthorne's personal life suggests the value he attached to domestic resolution in his tales. Yet it proved difficult to counter a profound vision of evil with a peaceful portrait of the fireside—especially in the tale, by definition a relatively short fictional form which promoted intensity rather than scope. In his romances, Hawthorne would strive more explicitly for a redemptive vision (though his blonde maidens, with their indestructible fraility, might seem to promise captivity rather than redemption). In the tales, however, he could do little more than assert the value of domesticity. His greatest achievement would come from his treatment of those who—for one reason or another—have become homeless.

Such, as the world knows, is the case of young Goodman Brown, who is exposed to the mightiest vision of evil Hawthorne ever imagined. Goodman Brown's journey into the forest is best defined as a kind of general, indeterminate allegory, representing man's irrational drive to leave faith, home, and security temporarily behind, for whatever reason, and take a chance with one (more) errand onto the wilder shores of experience. Our protagonist is an Everyman named Brown, a "young" man who will be aged by knowledge in one night. In the forest he goes through a dreamlike experience marked by a series of abrupt transitions and sudden apparitions. From the devil he learns that virtue is a dream, evil the only reality. And once Goodman Brown sees that idea in all its magnitude, he can never see anything else. He has withdrawn into the dream world of the forest, there to find a reality steeped in guilt that makes his return to the village a pilgrimage into untruth and hypocrisy. Into what he now sees as a flimsy community dream. From his vision in the forest, Goodman Brown receives a paralyzing sense of the brotherhood of man under the fatherhood of the devil. The thrust of Hawthorne's narrative is toward a climactic vision of universal evil, which leaves in its aftermath a stern legacy of distrust.

Robin Molineux also leaves home—for a different reason and with a different conclusion, of course, though he, too, encounters the fantastic and confronts a shocking vision.

In "My Kinsman, Major Molineux," as in "Young Goodman Brown," Hawthorne sets the conditions of his fiction so that they serve the purposes of his tale with maximum effectiveness. The strategy of the narrative employs Robin-in-history as a way of making us see history-in-Robin. Thus introjected, history affords the latitude of dream. Robin's mind vibrates between "fancy and reality." A feeling of homelessness accentuates his confusion. Locked out of the house of his memory, he has not yet been admitted to the house of his expectations. Thus, he occupies a middle ground, to which (as he sits in front of the church) "the moon, creating, like the imaginative power, a beautiful strangeness in familiar objects, gave something of romance to a scene that might not have possessed it in the light of day." The procession that passes in front of him has "a visionary air, as if a dream had broken loose from some feverish brain, and were sweeping visibly through the midnight streets." The nightmare has indeed broken loose; Robin can no longer avoid seeing it for what it is. At the center of the wild procession, enshrined in "tar-and-feather dignity," sits the Major. The two look at each other in silence, "and Robin's knees shook, and his hair bristled, with a mixture of pity and terror."

The identity Robin had hoped to establish by claiming kin has been swept away beyond recall. His laugh, cathartic and sanative, signifies that the passage from dream to nightmare to waking reality has been accomplished. Significantly, he does not repudiate the Major; to do so would be to succumb to the nightmare through which he has lived. But perhaps, as his new friend suggests, he may wish to remain in town and try to "rise in the world" without the Major's help. To succeed, Robin must put away the cudgel he has brought with him from the forest, dispense with the anticipated patronage of his kinsman, and establish his own identity in a society restively intent on doing the same.

A sense of homelessness likewise underlies the issues confronted in "The May-Pole of Merry Mount." "Jollity and gloom were contending for an empire," says Hawthorne in introducing the opposing forces in the tale. Most immediately at stake is the empire of two young hearts, which is, at the moment the Puritans rush forth, in a state of sadness and doubt. For the love of Edith and Edgar has wrought their moral and emotional estrangement from the community. The former Lord and Lady of the May have "no more a home at Merry Mount"; they have become subject to "doom, . . . sorrow, and troubled joy." It is as if their graduation from folly has evoked a stern adult world; the clash of Puritans and Merry Mounters becomes an imperial context for their emotional initiation into life. Again, the conditions of fiction are made functional to the tale: at twilight, from concealment, emerge the Puritans, whose "darksome figures were intermixed with the wild shapes of their foes," making the scene "a picture of the moment, when waking thoughts start up amid the scattered fantasies of a dream." The dream of

Merry Mount—the period of youth and play—is over; Edith and Edgar must now confront the waking—and adult—world. And again, as in "My Kinsman, Major Molineux," a double context: Hawthorne has played out a private drama of maturation in the context of tensions inherent in New England history—just as he has played out a drama of New England history in the more intimate yet more expansive context of awakening love.

A MODE OF CREATION

"Young Goodman Brown," "My Kinsman, Major Molineux," and "The May-Pole of Merry Mount" demonstrate that Hawthorne's need to establish the conditions of fiction could be made to serve the fiction itself. But if the requirements of Hawthorne's imagination called for a neutral ground as a way of conceiving the tale (which traditionally allowed for a heightened presentation of reality), they called also for a mode of creation that would impregnate his work with relevance for the moral condition of mankind. What Hawthorne had to say about sin, isolation, and the desiccating effects of idea came from his conception of a blemished human nature. To articulate his vision of "what prisoners we are," he frequently made use of an allegorical mode, shaping his materials so that they would suggest the contours of an outer and moral reality.

Although his tales reflect an allegorical tendency, Hawthorne was not a master allegorist. In later years he looked with disfavor on his "blasted allegories" (among which he probably included his processionals), the thinness of which caused Melville to say that Hawthorne needed to frequent the butcher, that he ought to have "roast beef done rare." He made use of conventional devices, giving his characters such names as Gathergold and Dryasdust, conceiving them generically as the Cynic and the Seeker, and envisioning his material so that it would illuminate a general truth of the moral world. Typically, he makes apparent his allegorical intent. He asks specifically, we recall, that "The Threefold Destiny" be read as an allegory; he notes that "Egotism; or, the Bosom Serpent" and "The Christmas Banquet" come "from the unpublished 'Allegories of the Heart' "; and he constructs "The Celestial Rail-Road" on the classic allegorical foundation bequeathed by Bunyan in *Pilgrim's Progress*. An allegorical tradition afforded Hawthorne a means of access to the moral world. Because the moral world was essential to his vision of humanity, he brought features of that tradition to bear on the form of the tale.

Hawthorne's most significant adaptation of an allegorical mode can be seen in his habit of presenting bifurcated or fragmented characters who complement each other in the totality of an individual tale. Such characters require, even as they contribute to, the kind of latitude which Hawthorne constantly strove to attain. More than this: by means of the configuration of such characters, Hawthorne confronts themes that define the specific nature of his work. He suggests in a number of tales, for example (and in a manner distinct from that of his processionals), the uncertain relationship between the man of imagination and the man of practicality. In "The Artist of the Beautiful" (1844), the scorn, practical strength, and shallow sensibility of the world (represented respectively by Peter Hovenden, Robert Danforth, and Annie) victimize the artist who must work, if he is to work, out of a determined *mésalliance* to society. As an artist Owen Warland succeeds; he succeeds even more significantly by being able to transcend the destruction of his creation. But he is forced into, even as he willingly adopts, a position of asociality or even anti-sociality if he is to create at all. In "Peter Goldthwaite's Treasure" (1837), the man of business saves the man of fancy from utter ruin. At one (ideal?) time, Peter Goldthwaite and John Brown have been in partnership; after the partnership dissolves, Peter goes through years of foolish hopes and financial disasters, finally tearing down his house in a vain effort to find legendary wealth. John Brown, meanwhile, prospers unspectacularly. No doubt John Brown is dull, unexciting, and basically unimaginative; but he rescues Peter Goldthwaite, arrests a career of sterility and self-destruction, and promises to protect the man of deluded imagination from his own fantasies. When John Brown plays the role of Mr. Lindsey in "The Snow-Image" (1850), however, he is blind to all but common sense. In caustic language, Hawthorne tells us how Mr. Lindsey completely overrides the high imaginative faith of his wife. Unable to withstand his bleak, unknowing, factual stare, the marvelous melts away before his eyes without his realizing that he has played the role of antagonist in a diminutive tragedy of the imagination. In each of these tales, and in others—such as "The Birthmark" (1843)—as well, a configuration of fragmented characters defines the theme and constitutes a wholeness of effect.

Hawthorne found aspects of an allegorical mode useful in articulating his sense of the complexities of the human condition. But the symbolic mode could also involve moral considerations and at the same time offer great flexibility and economy to the writer of tales. Inheriting a penchant for symbolism from the Puritans, disposed, too, toward symbolic expression by the exigencies of the creative situation in his society, Hawthorne came to place dramatic emphasis on the symbol as a way of achieving effective form in the tale. By means of the symbol he could portray the ambivalence of motive and the ambiguity of experience that defined for him the texture of the human condition. Mr. Hooper's black veil, for example, isolates the minister, who sees, simply and profoundly, that all men wear such veils. Feared by his parishioners, shunned by children, Mr. Hooper nonetheless preaches with power and efficacy. The veil is Mr. Hooper's "parable"; it proclaims the truth that all men hide the truth. But Hawthorne's parable suggests the divisive nature of such a truth and the ultimate failure of an eloquence that can illuminate everything but its source.

The symbol for Hawthorne promoted narrative focus and intensity even as it allowed for economy of presentation. Moreover, and with significant formal consequences, it proved possible to organize a tale effectively in terms of one central symbol. One symbol dominates "The Minister's Black Veil." The Maypole commands the focus of "The May-Pole of Merry Mount." And other well-known tales (written between 1836 and 1850) are structured in a similar way, among them "The Great Carbuncle," "Lady Eleanore's Mantle," "The Birthmark," "The Artist of the Beautiful," and "The Great Stone Face." Finally, of course, there is *The Scarlet Letter,* the culmination of Hawthorne's efforts to adapt the form of the tale to the special purposes of his imagination.

With its sustained tone and rigid economy of presentation; its use of the past and concern for the "great warm heart of the people"; its ambivalence, mode of characterization, and exploration of the protean nature of pride; and, above all, its use of a central symbol to generate narrative coherence, *The Scarlet Letter* is the master product of the method of Hawthorne's tales. In *The Scarlet Letter,* he extended the form of the tale until the suppressed imaginative energy of the narrative threatened to make it into something different. *The Scarlet Letter* marks Hawthorne's final accomplishment in the tale even as it signals the beginning of his achievement in the romance; it marks the point at which Hawthorne transformed the tale into the romance in his effort to adapt that form once again to the purposes of his imagination.

The presence of "The Custom-House" in *The Scarlet Letter* is of crucial importance. Afraid that his tale of the scarlet letter would prove too somber by itself, Hawthorne included "The Custom-House" as a way of lightening the tone of his volume. As a form, the sketch had been extremely useful to Hawthorne; it had long given him a way to deal with the present, the immediate, the actual—the very things he had to evade or attenuate for the purposes of his fiction. Hawthorne tended to sketch what was recalcitrant to his imagination. In turn, the sketch became an avenue to the world around him. This we can see in (among other sketches) "Sights from a Steeple" (1830), in "Night Sketches: Beneath an Umbrella" (1837), and in his extremely effective "The Old Manse" (1846). The narrator of "Night Sketches," having given a day to fancy, finds "a gloomy sense of unreality" depressing his spirits and impelling him to venture out in order to satisfy himself "that the world is not entirely made up of such shadowy materials as have busied me throughout the day." Through the medium of the sketch, he re-establishes contact with the world.

The world of the Salem Custom House, Hawthorne tells us, was stultifying to his imagination. He could neither write fiction while he worked there nor treat fictionally of the Custom House afterwards. But he could and did *sketch* the life of the Custom House in a memorable way. And he wedded the sketch and the tale, the present and the past, by his claim of having found the scarlet letter in the attic of the Custom House. In "The Old Manse," Hawthorne had told of exploring the garret of the Manse, which was "but a twilight at the best," and finding manuscripts and other records of former generations. In "The Custom-House," he develops the fullest possibilities of the idea of finding a document and becoming an editor. And his sketch now served the purposes of his fiction; it provided a way to reflect prefatorily on the past, to define the neutral ground as the basis of imaginative creation, and to introduce the fiction by claiming to have found it shunted aside into a corner of the present world. Uniquely and memorably, the sketch established the conditions of fiction in *The Scarlet Letter*.

In later years, Hawthorne's method of integrating past and present in *The Scarlet Letter* must have appealed strongly to him. He planned, for example, to preface *The Ancestral Footstep* with a sketch of his consular experiences at Liverpool in which he would hear from a visitor the legendary story that would constitute his romance. *Septimius Felton* was to be prefaced with a sketch of Hawthorne's residence at the Wayside which would introduce the legend Hawthorne had heard from Thoreau of the man who would not die: "I may fable that a manuscript was found," wrote Hawthorne in a preliminary study of *Septimius,* "containing records of this man, and allusions to his purposes to live forever." Finally, Hawthorne intended that *The Dolliver Romance* would begin with a prefatory sketch of Thoreau, during the course of which Hawthorne would mention the legend that was to be the theme of the romance.

During these years, when he was writing with difficulty and indecision, Hawthorne thus attempted to blend past and present as he had done so brilliantly in *The Scarlet Letter*. The form of the sketch, he hoped, would again contain and yield his fiction, as "The Custom-House" had contained and yielded the scarlet letter. But Hawthorne in the 1860's was working at cross purposes: in the late romances, potentially symbolic objects remained devoid of meaning or else labored under a significance arbitrarily assigned to them; bursts of inventiveness lacked direction and were followed by periods of acute dissatisfaction; "the Present, the Immediate, the Actual" could not be made to accommodate the past, the remote, and the imaginary—and no sketch could of itself bear the full burden of creation. *The Scarlet Letter,* in which after more than two decades as an author Hawthorne made his greatest sketch serve the purposes of his greatest tale, remained a unique achievement, one not to be duplicated.

Daniel Hoffman

Yankee Bumpkin and Scapegoat King

I

"In youth, men are apt to write more wisely than they really know
or feel; and the remainder of life may be not idly spent in realizing and
convincing themselves of the wisdom which they uttered long ago."
This reflection occurred to Hawthorne as he gathered his fugitive writings of two decades for *The Snow-Image, and Other Twice-Told Tales.*
The very last of these, whether so placed as a capstone or an after-
thought, proves to be his earliest full success and and one of the most
durable and contemporary fictions of his entire career. "My Kinsman,
Major Molineux" is unusual among Hawthorne's writings in its overt
treatment of the most important political and cultural problem of the
American republic: self-determination and its consequences. The tale is
striking, too, in its bold and direct appropriation from folk traditions
and popular culture of the representative traits of the New England
character. Hawthorne would use these humorously in "Mr.
Higginbotham's Catastrophe," ironically in portraying Holgrave in *The
House of the Seven Gables,* and descriptively in his war-time account of
President Lincoln. But now, in 1831, he anticipates by a quarter-
century Melville's use of similar materials and themes in "Benito
Cereno" and *The Confidence-Man* to attack the popular doctrines of
optimism and self-reliance which those traditions themselves exemp-
lify. In "My Kinsman, Major Molineux" these folk themes are placed
in dramatic opposition to an eighteenth-century Colonial reenactment of
the ancient ritual of the deposition of the Scapegoat King. This ritual
occurs in the story as the fulfillment of the hero's quest for his influen-

tial kinsman; its function, in terms of his own development, is to provide a ceremony of initiation. What is revealed to him is self-knowledge far deeper than his callow folk-character had hitherto anticipated.

In Hawthorne's tale, a youth named Robin, now eighteen and thinking it "high time to begin the world," sets out from his father's farm on his "first visit to town." There, with the help of Major Molineux, his father's cousin, he expects to make his fortune. Thus Robin is on the threshold of metamorphosis, like young Ben Franklin walking up Market Street with a loaf of bread under his arm. Committed to upward mobility, he is as yet dependent upon benevolent, paternalistic authority. As he becomes "entangled in a succession of crooked and narrow streets" his quest for his kinsman brings him only bafflement and mocking laughter from every quarter: from a ridiculously solemn old man, from a barber, an innkeeper, a demoniac fiery-eyed patron at the inn, a trollop in a scarlet petticoat, a watchman. Parties of men approach, speak to him in gibberish, and when he cannot answer curse him in plain English. In desperation Robin accosts a muffled burly stranger with his cudgel and demands to be directed to his kinsman. Instead of forcing his passage the man says, "Watch here an hour, and Major Molineux will pass by." With a start Robin recognizes the demoniac of the inn. "One side of the face blazed an intense red, while the other was black as midnight . . . as if two individual devils, a fiend of fire and a fiend of darkness, had united themselves to form this infernal visage." Now, waiting by moonlight on the church steps, Robin thinks of the home he has left. In a reverie he sees his father giving the family blessings: "Then he saw them go in at the door; and when Robin would have entered also, the latch tinkled into place, and he was excluded from his home." He dreams—or wakes—to see his kinsman's face regarding him from a nearby window. Waking in truth, he asks a passing stranger whether he must wait all night for Major Molineux. The stranger, a mature, prepossessing man, "perceiving a country youth, apparently homeless and without friends . . . accosted him in a tone of real kindness." When Robin tells his mission the gentleman replies, "I have a singular curiosity to witness your meeting," and sits beside him. Soon sounds of a Saturnalia approach, then a wild procession headed by the double-faced man, who watches Robin the while, swirls past by torch-light, drawing a cart. "There, in tar-and-feathery dignity, sat his kinsman, Major Molineux!"

> He was an elderly man, of large and majestic person, and strong, square features, betokening a steady soul; but steady as it was, his enemies had

found means to shake it. . . . But perhaps the bitterest pang of all was when his eyes met those of Robin; for he evidently knew him on the instant, as the youth stood witnessing the foul disgrace of a head grown grey in honor. They stared at each other in silence, and Robin's knees shook, and his hair bristled, with a mixture of pity and terror.

Then, one by one, the laughing mockers of his night-long adventure add their derisive voices to the din. "The contagion . . . all at once seized upon Robin . . . Robin's shout was the loudest there." At the leader's signal, "On they went, like fiends that throng in mockery around some dead potentate, mighty no more, but majestic still in his agony . . . and left a silent street behind." Robin's companion lays a hand on his shoulder. "Well, Robin, are you dreaming?" Robin, "his eye not quite as lively as in the earlier part of the evening," replies by asking to be shown the way to the ferry. "I grow weary of town life, sir." But this friendly stranger declines to oblige him, suggesting that "If you prefer to remain with us, perhaps, as you are a shrewd youth, you may rise in the world without the help of your kinsman, Major Molineux."

From even this crude précis of the plot it is hard to take seriously Parrington's strictures against Hawthorne as a mere romancer of the murky past who avoided dealing with the problems and issues of Jacksonian democracy. One of the two chief interpretations of "My Kinsman, Major Molineux," that of Q. D. Leavis,[1] suggests how deeply involved Hawthorne was with the basic problems of American self-realization. She sees this tale as "a symbolic action which . . . takes the form of something between a pageant and a ritual drama, disguised in the emotional logic of a dream." She suggests that the tale be subtitled "America Comes of Age," and reads it as an historic parable in which Robin "represents the young America" who has come to town, "that is, the contemporary scene where the historic future will be decided." The opening paragraphs of the tale establish that popular insurrections and violent deaths of the governors were characteristic of the history of the colonies.

A quite different reading is suggested by Hyatt H. Waggoner and elaborated by Roy R. Male.[2] Waggoner emphasizes the dreamlike manipulation of incident, sound, and color in the tale, and reads its primary meaning as a revelation of an Oedipal conflict. The tale reveals "man's image of himself as the destroyer of the father—because he has wished

---

[1] "Hawthorne as Poet" [Part I], *Sewanee Review,* LIX (Spring 1951), 198–205.

[2] Waggoner, *Hawthorne, A Critical Study* (Cambridge, 1955), pp. 47–53; Male, *Hawthorne's Tragic Vision* (Austin, Tex., 1957), pp. 48–53.

the destruction—a destroyer bathed in guilt yet somehow justified. . . .
Passing through the stages of initial identification with the father image,
rejection, and shame, Robin at last emerges with the help of the stranger
into maturity." Male's elaboration of this Freudian reading suggests
"that visions of the father figure may commonly be split into two or
more images." The pompous old man and the watchman then "are
shapes of what Robin is attempting to leave behind." Other figures are
"various forms of the cultured kinsman he is seeking."

> Thus as he verges upon maturity the young man's yearnings for freedom
> from authority and for a worldly patrimony take on exaggerated propor-
> tions. The dual aspect of this psychic conflict can be seen in the "infernal
> visage" of the "double-faced fellow," whose complexions are split. . . .
> The grotesque fusion of the two forms is a distorted father image in which
> youthful misrepresentation of both the real father and the real uncle are
> combined.

Robin's real father appears in his dream of home, and again as the
kindly stranger who stays by his side during the imaged destruction of
Major Molineux. The kinsman, of course, is the most potent father-
image in the story.

II

The truth of the tale includes both these theories and more.
Hawthorne's most successful fictions may be described by a phrase
from one of his least effective stories: "I can never separate the idea
from the symbol in which it manifests itself."[3] In his best tales, simple
arrangements of objects, persons, or actions are the symbols, but these
are so economically chosen as to represent complex constellations of
ideas. Certainly the pattern of action in "My Kinsman, Major
Molineux" is at the same time a journey, a search, an initiation. Robin
is indeed a representative American, first as witness, then as partici-
pant, in a cultural-political experience of archetypal significance to our
national identity. He is also a representative young man who must come
to terms with his feelings about his father, about the past, about authority, in order to pass from adolescence into maturity.

In psychological terms, Male is probably right that all the men in

[3] "The Antique Ring," *Works,* XII, 67.

the story are displacements or substitutions for the father, in his several aspects: as authority (to be feared, courted, or ridiculed), and as paternity (to be loved, escaped from, and depended upon). But there are other implications necessary to a full involvement with the tale. Major Molineux is not only the Father as Authority, he is also the Past which must be rejected. Specifically, he represents British rule—in political terms he is the representative of the Crown. If psychologically the Major displaces Robin's father, politically and culturally he actually displaces the King. As authority figure, whether patristic or regal, he represents Order, Tradition, Stability. But as the Father-King in a cart whose "tar-and-feathery dignity" inspires the tragic emotions of pity and terror, Major Molineux takes on yet further dimensions. He is the Sacrificed King, the Royal Scapegoat, the "dead potentate . . . majestic still in his agony" around whom the townsfolk "throng in mockery." Frazer analyzes the Scapegoat King as a ritual role invested with two functions, the expulsion of evil and the sacrificial death of the divine ruler whose declining potency is renewed in his young successor. One can hardly suggest that this modern anthropological theory was available to Hawthorne in 1831, but from his tale we can infer his intuitive understanding of the primitive ritual which he used metaphorically in describing the downfall of Major Molineux. The rebellion in the tale, although dated vaguely around 1730, is clearly a "type" of the American Revolution. This was indeed the supercession of an older order by a new, from which ensued a revitalization of the energies of American society. Hawthorne remarks that the colonists had frequently attacked the person of their royal governors, however suppliant to their demands the governors, as individuals, had been. In this there is the inference that in tarring and feathering Major Molineux the conspirators are symbolically ridding the colony of a symbol of the chief evil that prepossessed their consciousness as a culture. Further warrant for inferring Major Molineux to represent a Scapegoat King is suggested by one of the identities of his antagonist, the man with the double visage.

This character may be, as Male proposes, a double father-image combining "youthful misrepresentation of both the real father and the real uncle." Yet we must also take him more literally than this; or, if we take him in metaphors, let the metaphors be Hawthorne's own. He is described as both "a fiend of fire and a fiend of darkness," and, when he rides on horseback at the head of the ceremonial procession, "his fierce and variegated countenance appeared like war personified; the red of one cheek was an emblem of fire and sword; the blackness of the other betokened the mourning that attends them.'' He is War, Death, and Destruction, and again he is the Devil, with "his train [of] wild figures in Indian dress," his "infernal visage," and his eyes that glowed "like fire in a cave.'' He is well chosen to play the part of Riot, of Disorder, of the Lord of Misrule, in the pageant it is Robin's destiny to behold. He is in charge of the procession of "fiends" and of their lurid rites, the "counterfeited pomp," the "senseless uproar" in which the tumultuous multitude lead Major Molineux to his humiliation.

And Robin joins this yelling mob! His mocking laughter is the loudest there! Not even the shame, the agony of his kinsman, not even his own emotions of pity and terror, can hold him from making their "frenzied merriment" his own. There are buffetings of passion, there are possibilities of evil and of guilt, which Robin's callow rationalism cannot fathom. Setting out merely to make his way in the world, he has wandered unknowingly toward an appointed rendezvous, a ceremony which seems to have been prepared specifically for his benefit. It is his initiation.

But an initiation into what? The sensitive suggestions of Mrs. Leavis, Waggoner, and Male may be supplemented by a closer scrutiny of Robin himself. When we have seen who he is and what he represents up to the moment of his initiation, we can better understand the significance of that ritual for him.

Seven times in this tale Robin is characterized as "a shrewd youth." Like his antecedent bumpkins in popular tradition—Brother Jonathan, the peddlers of folk anecdote, Jack Downing, Sam Slick—he is nothing if not shrewd. But Robin is shrewd only by his own report. "I'm not the fool you take me for," he warns the double-faced demon, yet that is exactly what he is. Although mystified at every turn, denied the common civilities by those he meets, taunted and mocked by strangers at the mention of his kinsman's name, he never once loses confidence in his own shrewdness. Rebuffed by the pompous old man and the innkeeper, fleeing the temptations of the prostitute, his response to their jeering laughter is thrice again to account himself "a shrewd youth." Even in his last encounter with the stranger who proves to be kindly, Robin is still depending on his motherwit to carry him through all situations. "For I have the name of being a shrewd youth," Robin tells his older friend. "I doubt not that you deserve it," the friend replies. Yet at the beginning of his night of misadventure Robin had stepped jauntily off the ferry without realizing that he had no idea where he was going. "It would have been wise to inquire my way of the ferryman," he muses, "But the next man I meet will do as well." This, however, is not at all the case. Everyone he meets is, unknown to him, involved in the conspiracy to overthrow his kinsman the royal governor. When Robin cannot give their password, parties of conspirators curse him in plain language. When he obstinately inquires for the Major the people in the inn and the barbershop hoot at him. When he tries the door of the pretty little prostitute she tells him that she knows his kinsman well. "But Robin, being of the household of a New England clergyman, was a good youth, as well as a shrewd one; so he resisted temptation, and fled away." He cannot yet face the knowledge that Major Molineux, his kinsman (and father), has had carnal knowledge of a woman, just as Young Goodman Brown will be dismayed to learn that his father had followed the Devil to the witches' carnal Sabbath before him.

It is characteristic of Robin that he always accepts the most simplistic rationalizations of the most baffling and ominous experiences. One would think him affrighted by the demoniac double-faced man he accosts before the church. We recognize this portentous apparition as ringleader of the uprising, but Robin merely muses, "Strange things we travellers see!" and sits down to await the Major. "A few moments were consumed in philosophical speculations upon the species of man who had just left him; but having settled this point shrewdly, rationally, and satisfactorily, he was compelled to look elsewhere for his amusement"! Now the moonlight plays over the commonplace scene "like the imaginative power," and Robin cannot define the forms of distant objects which turn ghostly and indistinct "just as his eye appeared to grasp them." His dream of home is more real than the actual things he is now among, and when he wakes "his mind kept vibrating between fancy and reality" as shapes lengthen and dwindle before him. Despite all these physical sensations of confusion and the constant evidence of his noncomprehension of what is happening, Robin trusts to his "name of being a shrewd youth." This is Yankee self-reliance with a vengeance! His "bright, cheerful eyes were nature's gifts," and he would seem to think he needs no others. Robin, the shrewd youth from the backwoods, proves to be the Great American Boob, the naïf whose odyssey leads him, all uncomprehending, into the dark center of experience.

When the tale opens, Robin has just made a crossing of the water and entered the city. He has left behind him the security as well as the simplicity of his rural birthplace—in his reverie before the church his country home seemed an Arcadian bower of "venerable shade" and "golden light." But in his dream of returning home the door closes before him. Like Wakefield, Robin has left his home and cannot return. It is true that, as opposed to Wakefield's perverse impulse, he had good reasons (Robin is a younger son and won't inherit the farm), but nonetheless by leaving his appointed place and station to participate in the fluidity of egalitarian city life he too has made himself an exile. Just how egalitarian that city life will prove Robin must learn with dismay. The change to which he has committed himself is not only one of place and status but involves also the breaking of human ties, as every act of independence does to some degree. Much as Robin resembles the folk characters of Yankee yarn and jokelore, the difference—and it is tremendous—is that such characters had no human ties to break.

Robin's journey toward independence is magnified a thousand-fold by the throes of the town itself on the evening of his arrival. In their quest for self-determination the urban conspirators of the town are far in advance of the country-bred youth whom they mock. Until the very end of the tale Robin still counts on his kinsman's preferment; the independence he seeks is therefore qualified, not absolute. The townsfolk no longer accept the limited independence granted by royal governors, even those who "in softening their instructions from beyond the sea . . . incurred the reprehension" of the Crown. They have cast their die for total disseverance of their bonds. Hawthorne's imagery puts them in league with the Devil to do so.

Thus an ironic tension underlies all of Robin's misadventures. Those who deride him are really his mentors, and he, invoking the patronage of their enemy his kinsman, is actually their ally, since both they and he are seeking independence. After his dismay at beholding his kinsman's degradation, Robin's sudden shout of laughter may seem to the reader inexplicable. So it is, from a point of view as rational and "shrewd" as his own. But the emotional logic that produced his outburst is inescapable. It is an emotional not a rational logic, for in that instant, with neither premeditation nor understanding, Robin has cast off the remaining dependence of his immaturity.

Then, at the Devil's behest, the frenzied procession moves on, leaving Robin behind in the silent street. What has he learned from his initiation?

His lessons must be inferred from the tale, for when it ends Robin is still in a state of shock. "I begin to grow weary of town life," he says. He wants to go home. But, as his dream has already told him, he has no home now. He must stay. What he might muse on is his new knowledge of the demonic depths from which the impulse to self-determination leaped up in the torchlight. He might give "a few moments" in "philosophical speculations" upon the Saturnalian passions which shook him as he, like the populace, dethroned Order and rejected

Tradition while under the aegis of the Lord of Misrule. In their act of revolt they have all thrown down the old king of Stability and crowned the new prince of War and Destruction.

To judge from the effect upon Robin of his experiences hitherto, there is little chance of his learning much from these reflections. Although devoted to the dogma of Yankee self-reliance, he had learned nothing from anything that had touched him. We are, however, told that his faith in himself is rather shaken, for "nature's gift," his "bright, cheerful eyes," are now "not quite as lively as in the earlier part of the evening."

One source of hope for Robin is the continued interest of the gentleman who had befriended him. This nameless figure, as we have seen, represents the viable influence of his father upon his soul: the manly guidance of a non-possessive, non-inhibiting paternal love. The tale ends with the steadying voice of this personage, whose interested detachment from the pillorying of Major Molineux hints that he has seen all this before. In his experience he knows that this ritual, like all *rites de passage,* is ever again repeated for the benefit of each initiate. Even his irony at the end is indulgent without being patronizing, for he suggests that Robin will have to make up his own mind, "as you are a shrewd youth," whether to stay in town and "perhaps . . . rise in the world without the help of your kinsman, Major Molineux," even though he surely knows that Robin cannot return to his pastoral home. This means that Robin now is free of the past, and has the power of self-determination. But this power comes to him inextricable from the terrifying and tragic emotions that have involved him.

And what of the Colony? Is it truly free, or has it exchanged the rule of a benevolent governor for the tyranny of riot and chaos? On the political level Hawthorne's fable is less reassuring than on the personal. There is no double of Major Molineux who represents in the realm of power what Robin's friend stands for as an aspect of the parent. Yet so closely has Hawthorne intertwined the cultural with the psychological implications in this tale that we cannot help taking Robin's friend as representing also the viable aspects of Major Molineux. What his patient and tolerant advice to Robin suggests, then, is that this ordeal has been performed before by society as well as by the self. The implication is that the forces of Order and Stability do in the end prove stronger than those of Destruction and Misrule which dethrone them. Harrowing though these disruptive forces be, in Hawthorne's vision of American history they do serve the end of re-establishing a stable order based on institutions more just than those overthrown. (This was in fact the case, as the fire-brained Committees of Correspondence were superseded, after the reign of War and Death, by the framers of the Constitution and the *Federalist Papers*.[4]) Still another indication that the reign of Riot will be but brief lies in the carnival atmosphere which suggests that Major Molineux's successor, the two-faced man, is the Lord of Misrule. His reign is but a mock reign, a temporary season of emotional debauch necessary to the purification and rebirth of society. At its conclusion Order is imposed again upon the rampaging passions of the Saturnalia. On this succession the continuity of culture itself depends. In "My Kinsman," then, there is a qualified, half-skeptical hope that when the town wakes up from its collective nightmare, tradition will be re-established in accordance with the new dispensation of absolute liberty which the Devil's league had won in the darkness.

But as in the case of Robin's personal fate, the consequences of these public actions are not affirmed, not even proposed. All consequences are but inferences from this fable. Our inferences must be guided by the probabilities which the characterization of Robin in terms of the traditional figure of the Yankee naïf suggests. There is no clearer statement in our literature than "My Kinsman, Major Molineux" of the psychological and cultural burdens of personal freedom and of national independence. Hawthorne's Robin allows us no undue confidence in the degree of understanding with which the American character will bear them.

---

[4]If the spirit of revolt is in this tale a Devil, he appears elsewhere in Hawthorne as "The Gray Champion," the regicide Goffe who signed King Charles's death warrant. "His hour is one of darkness, and adversity, and peril. But should domestic tyranny oppress us . . . still may the Gray Champion come, for he is the type of New England's hereditary spirit." There, as in "Legends of the Province House" and "Endicott and the Red Cross," rebellion is the divine right of an oppressed people.

J. Donald Crowley

The Unity of Hawthorne's Twice-Told Tales

I

Writing to Longfellow on March 7, 1837, the day the first edition of *Twice-Told Tales* was published, Hawthorne, in his typically self-deprecatory way, apologized for inflicting his " 'twice-told' tediousness" on his old college acquaintance and then went on to remark that "The present volume contains such articles as seemed best worth offering to the public a second time." For that collection, the first book to carry his name on the title page, he selected eighteen of the forty-three tales and sketches which had been published separately—and anonymously or pseudonymously—in newspapers, magazines, and gift-book annuals during the previous six years. There is nothing to suggest that nineteenth-century readers saw any reason to quarrel with Hawthorne's choices, and as late as 1939 the collection was described as one which, "though small, was thoroughly representative, and gave an accurate impression of Hawthorne's manner in its then modest range. It was a fair and favorable presentation." More recent critics have had other views, however, perhaps best summed up in what one has called the need to explain "that still astonishing phenomenon, the *Twice-Told Tales.*"

The *Twice-Told Tales* is "astonishing" even at this late date, but not because so much has been written about the collection *per se*— almost nothing has. The volumes have only recently become a point of critical bewilderment. Not having discovered "My Kinsman, Major

From Studies in American Fiction, *1 (Spring, 1973), 35–62. Copyright © 1973 by Northeastern University. Revised by the author for publication here and reprinted by permission. (The original essay also treated the unity of the 1842 edition.)*

Molineux" until the 1950s, critics realized as if for the first time that, although Hawthorne had written the tale before 1830, he did not see fit to acknowledge it until 1851 when he hastily gathered together nearly all his vagrant, half-forgotten pieces for *The Snow-Image, and Other Twice-Told Tales*. This discovery in turn led quickly to a heightened sense of the discrepancy between the date of composition and first separate printing of other tales and their inclusion in a collection. Why did the 1837 and 1842 volumes not contain Hawthorne's other highly prized tales, "Roger Malvin's Burial," first printed in the *Token* for 1832, and "Young Goodman Brown," which appeared initially in the *New-England Magazine* in April, 1835? The question is finally unanswerable, but it has had embarrassing implications for most Hawthorne scholars, given the fact that, among other pieces in the two volumes, Hawthorne selected what are to modern taste such obviously inferior and disappointing ones as, say, "Little Annie's Ramble," "David Swan," "The Vision of the Fountain," "The Sister Years," and "Edward Fane's Rosebud". Indeed, some readers find it difficult to believe that the same man who could write "Molineux" could also have written many of the other tales. "And yet, when all is said and done," comments one, "there is much about Hawthorne that is unsatisfactory. . . . There remain *The Scarlet Letter* and a handful of stories. And there remains the question: why are they so good and the rest so bad?" If Hawthorne's remark to Longfellow in 1837 is a basically accurate and reliable statement of his assessment of his own work, his selection of tales and sketches for *Twice-Told Tales* illustrates dramatically the radical difference between the value he put on his work and the assessment modern criticism has most often made of it.

One dimension of the excellence he sought—and, like some of the other dimensions, felt he never quite achieved—is manifest in *Twice-Told Tales*. It arises out of certain of his assumptions about the requirements and the limitations of his fiction that are alien to those assumptions made by his critics. Central among these is what I would call his instinctive way of viewing his tales and sketches aggregately. Modern critics, quite understandably, have, in their desire to define and interpret the "classical" Hawthorne canon, focused to a remarkable degree on the individual achievement of the best tales. The very intensity of this enterprise, however, has almost precluded the possibility of examining the question of the tales considered collectively. The question is a difficult one, immersed as it is in the most problematic elements of Hawthorne's art and leading as it does to numerous other questions finally unanswerable. It involves, first of all, the complex problem of reconstructing Hawthorne's estimation of his tales and sketches in 1837 and 1842, an estimation we might reasonably expect to be different from the one he expresses later in the 1851 preface after the success of *The Scarlet Letter* allowed him to put behind him forever the agonies of writing magazine fiction and to luxuriate somewhat in denigrating his earlier work. However astute this reconstruction, there is little hope that we can ever finally account for all of Hawthorne's choices for those collections. The very nature of his work—the similarity between some of the pieces he chose and some he left out—prohibits that sort of evaluation. But the question is nevertheless a necessary and compelling one, and asking it leads also to a larger understanding of Hawthorne's art and to the possibility of seeing an integrity in the "inferior" tales without being forced to make extravagant claims for their formal splendor.

The view prevails that Hawthorne, having been unsuccessful in his efforts to publish three "unified" collections—"Seven Tales of My Native Land," "Provincial Tales," and "The Story Teller"—resorted wearily to something like disconnected catch-alls in *Twice-Told Tales, Mosses from an Old Manse* (1846), and *The Snow-Image* (1851). A considerable amount of evidence, however, suggests, if indirectly, that this is a too hasty conclusion. To be fully understood, the three major collections must be seen, at some point or other, in the context of Hawthorne's entire work and, more specifically, in relation to his other collections, projected and actual. While there is, unfortunately, no direct evidence in his extant letters demonstrating that he looked upon *Twice-Told Tales* as a unified collection, there is an abundance of data which shows that almost every other collection he even thought about he cast in terms of some principle of unity. In 1838, for example, when he proposed to Longfellow that they collaborate on a book of fairy tales for children, his first thought was that there ought to be a "slender thread of story running through the book, as a connecting medium for the other stories." In 1841, with his first collection of juvenile fiction, *Grandfather's Chair,* Hawthorne says in his preface that he "endeavored to keep a distinct and unbroken thread of authentic history" by means of relating "the adventures of the chair, which form the machinery of the work." The following year he unified some more of what he called his "drudge-work," *Biographical Stories,* by means of a framework which told of the convalescence of a young boy suffering from an eye disorder. And in 1851, when planning *A Wonder-Book for Girls and Boys,* he again immediately formulated his unifying device: "As a frame-work, I shall have a young college student telling these stories to his cousins and brothers and sisters, during his vacations, sometimes at the fireside, sometimes in the woods and dells." He developed this plan fully, with interludes between each story. A year or so later, in *Tanglewood Tales,* he dropped the headlinks but still retained the student Eustace Bright as the narrator.

But it was not only for the collections of juvenile stories that Hawthorne can be said to have instinctively desired some sort of framework or unifying device. The four "Legends of the Province House," first printed in 1838 and 1839, make it clear that even after the publication of *Twice-Told Tales* he found the device of an explicit dramatic framework an inviting and useful—even necessary —component in his most serious short fiction.[1] "Egotism; or the Bosom Serpent" and "The Christmas Banquet," originally published in 1843 and 1844, carried the subtitle "From the Unpublished 'Allegories of the Heart.'" Nelson Adkins has speculated that "The Birth-Mark," "Rappaccini's Daughter," "Earth's Holocaust," "The Antique Ring," "Ethan Brand," as well as other pieces written during the early 1840s, Hawthorne might have intended to use along with the other two in a thematically unified collection. Again, writing to Evert A. Duyckinck in 1845 about the difficulty he was having with the piece intended to begin *Mosses,* Hawthorne says that it was his "purpose to construct a sort of frame-work, in this new story, for the series of stories already published, and to make the scene an idealization of our parsonage, and of the river close at hand, with glimmerings of my actual life—yet so transmogrified that the reader should not know what was reality and what fancy." "The Old Manse," then, he conceived to be an introductory sketch that would somehow unify tales and sketches written over a fifteen-year period and initially published separately in a variety of periodicals. Once more, in 1850, when he was still skeptical about publishing *The Scarlet Letter* by itself rather than as part of still another collection—this one to be called "Old-Time Legends, Together with Sketches Experimental and Ideal"—his remarks indicate that he habitually viewed radically disparate pieces in relation to one another. To James T. Fields he stated his fears with characteristic humor: "A hunter loads his gun with a bullet and several buckshot, and following his sagacious example, it was my purpose to conjoin the one long story with half a dozen shorter ones; so that, failing to kill the public outright with my biggest and heaviest lump of lead, I might have other chances with the smaller bits, individually, and in the aggregate." That final phrase—"individually, and in the aggregate"—might be dismissed as a

---

[1]For an enlightening analysis of Hawthorne's framework, see Julian Smith, "Hawthorne's *Legends of the Province House," Nineteenth-Century Fiction,* 24 (June, 1969), 31–44.

casual remark were it not for all the other evidence that suggests Hawthorne always aimed at a totality of effect from his shorter pieces. One of his reasons for doing so, as his "buckshot" theory testifies, is that throughout his career he suffered from an uncertainty about and lack of confidence in the merits of his tales, an affliction brought on by the unhappy conditions of periodical publication and popular taste. The point is that a unifying principle or device of some kind—explicit or implicit—plays a persistent and central role in Hawthorne's thinking about his short fiction.

The evidence does much to contradict the commonly held view that Hawthorne was so disappointed in the *New-England Magazine's* failure to publish "The Story Teller" in serial form that he threw over altogether the notion of publishing a unified collection. His format for that collection is only a more elaborate variation of later ones: "With each specimen will be given a sketch of the circumstances in which the story was told. Thus my airdrawn pictures will be set in frames perhaps more valuable than the pictures themselves, since they will be embossed with groups of characteristic figures, amid the lake and mountain scenery, the villages and fertile fields, of our native land." According to his sister-in-law, Elizabeth Peabody, Hawthorne complained that "he cared little for the stories afterwards, which had in their original place in The Story Teller a greater degree of significance." Given the fact that this bulky two-volume manuscript would have had to include most of the stories he had written and that nearly all of them would make their way into his major collections, the most realistic interpretation of his attitude would seem to be that he was dissatisfied not so much with the tales themselves as with their separate, fragmented magazine appearances. At any rate, a writer who could describe his "frames" as being more important than his "pictures" would clearly exercise great care not only in the selection but also the arrangement of those tales when three years later he at last had the chance to publish them in book form and escape the destructive exigencies of magazine publication.

When Hawthorne failed to find a publisher for his early projected collections, he did not put aside once and for all the idea of a "unified" collection: he only changed his concept of what that unity should or might be. Indeed, that concept had already undergone large changes within the projected collections themselves. By early 1834 he had given up the idea of a unity based on subject matter. The unity he tried out in "The Story Teller" was substantially different and strongly influenced, I suspect, by Washington Irving's narrative manner. It derived, as the title indicates, from the character of the narrator, "whose shiftings of fortune were to form the interludes and links between the separate stories.'' The pieces intended for this collection were as various as those in the major collections, and it was not the stories told—not the fiction itself—but the story teller, who, in his attitudes and adventures, successes and failures, provided the unifying principle. However unsuccessful the collection was, Hawthorne's shift away from a design based on similar historical materials to one based on broad rhetorical considerations marks, if not the beginning, the formal development of one of his best defined and most enduring techniques: the use of cautiously self-revelatory (and self-concealing) statements in his sketches and prefaces as helpful introductions into, and as guarantees of, the fictions themselves.

I am suggesting that what Hawthorne did explicitly in these various framing devices in earlier collections he attempted to do implicitly in the 1837 (and 1842) *Twice-Told Tales*. In his developed frameworks he postulated a variety of particularized audiences and created interludes which dealt, on the one hand, with the audience's response to the stories told and, on the other, with the relationship between the narrator and his audience as well as that between the narrator and his art. The leading concerns of all those frameworks are rhetorical as well as picturesque; they involve a dual, simultaneous focus on imaginative fictionality itself and on an audience privy to that fictionality. The figure of the artist, the narrator, is always there in the center as a mediator between these two. Hawthorne sought to give *Twice-Told Tales* a rhetorical coherence by virtue of his selection and arrangement of tales and sketches. The story they tell is one that arises out of the central problem Hawthorne seems to have seen himself facing as an American artist who wanted to be a genuinely popular writer. Those two volumes represent a kind of battleground on which Hawthorne tested as honestly as he could the possibilities of imaginative experience—now inviting, now dangerous—and the capacities of his audience to participate in them. In creating the collection, he tried to define the relationship between the spiritual realities represented by the imagination and the hard, material actuality of his present world. Forced by various circumstances to write for a magazine and gift-book audience, Hawthorne invariably saw the central problem of his art as the necessity to awaken an audience virtually maimed in its capacity to feel and imagine. Hawthorne used as a motto for his first projected collection the title of Wordsworth's little lyric, ''We Are Seven.'' The central situation of that poem, however bathetic to modern readers, apparently appealed strongly to Hawthorne because he recognized, in the juxtaposition of the little girl who ''sees'' and the common-sensical adult who would see but cannot, a type of his own predicament with his audience. The device he used in *Biographical*

Stories—the narration of stories to a young boy with bandaged eyes in order to help him "try to see . . . with [his] heart"—is nothing more nor less than a literal extension of the submerged rhetorical situation guiding Hawthorne's choice of title for the 1837 collection. George Parsons Lathrop, like other earlier readers, saw the title as "Possibly . . . suggested by that line, given to Lewis, the Dauphin, in 'King John':—'Life is as tedious as a twice-told tale. . . .' '' Citing only this much of the speech, however, emphasizes only Hawthorne's self-deprecation and weariness as an author. One has to include the line following to get the full force of Hawthorne's reference: "Life is as tedious as a twice-told tale/Vexing the dull ear of a drowsy man. . . ." Thoreau would "brag as lustily as chanticleer in the morning . . . if only to wake [his] neighbors up." Such was not Hawthorne's style, but there is in that style, for all its self-negation, a quiet assertiveness that meant to vex as much as possible the genteelly dull ears of the reading public. In pointing to the fact that he was telling the stories a second time Hawthorne was suggesting not merely that they had been around before but that he meant, this time, to tell them together, in book form, and in such a way as to satisfy what, in all his lack of confidence about the matter, he defined as the most pressing demands of his art.

One of Hawthorne's clearest statements of the rhetorical basis of his collections—his concern with the relation of his art to his audience—occurs in "The Custom-House." There, in his polar descriptions of himself and the Old Inspector, Hawthorne actually formulates his vision of the artist and his audience. Hawthorne is "a man who felt it to be the best definition of happiness to live throughout the whole range of his faculties and sensibilities." The "father of the Custom-House," however, who controls Hawthorne-the-surveyor's destiny as the popular audience influences Hawthorne-the-artist's, "possessed no power of thought, no depth of feeling, no troublesome sensibilities; nothing, in short, but a few commonplace instincts, which, aided by the cheerful temper that grew inevitably out of his physical well-being, did duty very respectably, and to general acceptance, in lieu of a heart." The relationship between the two figures is paradigmatic for Hawthorne's art, and it indicates the sort of coherence he was striving for in *Twice-Told Tales,* a collection for which he chose as wide a variety of tales and sketches as possible in order to exhibit "the whole range of his faculties and sensibilities" and thus capture the public's attention by means of the aggregate effect of the tales as a whole. Choosing the pieces for such an effect, he arranged them in a sequence that best fulfilled a cumulative design in which individual tales and sketches—and at times groups of them—were set side by side so as to comment on one another and thus

guide his readers' responses. So would he attempt ''to open an intercourse with the world'' by making what he later called ''the kingdom of
possibilities'' in fictionality more available to the wide general audience
he consciously set out to attract.

II

All this is to say that Hawthorne felt compelled for numerous
reasons to spend almost as much artistic energy in creating ways to
instruct his audience about how to read his fiction as he did in creating
the appropriate forms for the fictions themselves. Indeed, these two
impulses seem at times to be inseparable parts of the same creative
process with him, a process in which he continually tested the authenticity of fictionality itself. His normal strategy is evident as early as his
revision of ''Alice Doane'' as ''Alice Doane's Appeal'' (1835 *Token),*
a revision which unquestionably made his framework more important
than the story itself. It is uppermost, too, in ''Wakefield,'' where he
makes the donnée of the tale the very process by which he seems to
invent it before the reader's eyes and even with the reader's help.
Emerson points to this quality in Hawthorne's work when he complains
that ''Hawthorne invites his readers too much into his study, opens the
process before them. As if the confectioner should say to his customers
Now let us make the cake.'' Hawthorne's habitual definition of his role
as a mediator between his art and audience, fiction and actuality, is
quite pronounced in numerous stories. Less evident, it is still there as a
dialectical design in *Twice-Told Tales*.

The first two pieces in the 1837 volume, ''The Gray Champion''
and ''Sunday at Home,'' announce in several ways the polar opposites
that describe the thematic boundaries of the collection. ''The Gray
Champion,'' one of the finest of Hawthorne's simple historical tales,
introduces the reader to a distant American past and then to a radical,
legendary fictionality: ''the figure of an ancient man, who seemed to
have emerged from the people,'' standing between the ''religious multitude'' and ''the group of despotic rulers.'' Thrust into a scene drawn
from factual history, this ''stately form,'' appearing in the ''twilight
shadow'' which symbolizes Hawthorne's ''neutral territory,'' gives expression to the aspirations of the oppressed colonists; and his presence,
reminding them of their past (just as the tale itself is to remind
Hawthorne's readers of their past), creates in them a steadfast sense of
the community and common destiny to be won. ''Sunday at Home''

provides a dramatic contrast to the historical tale not only in its form
—that of the meditative sketch—but in its characters, subject, theme,
and point of view. Here, instead of the focus being on a distant past
where the "Actual" and the "Imaginary" can meet and on a legendary
national hero who is "the type of New England's heriditary spirit," it is
on the isolated narrator who looks out from behind the curtain of his
open window onto the world of contemporary actuality. In the tale the
eyes of friend and foe alike are focused intensely, unbelievingly on a
single, mysterious object; in the sketch, the single, withdrawn narrator
glances down in a relatively leisurely fashion on the various people who
make up the church congregation. The situation of Hawthorne's persona here is, of course, a complete inversion of the gray champion's:
the legendary figure, positioned between hostile forces, arouses a spirit
of democratic solidarity, but the narrator of the sketch, a spectator only,
having no effect on what he observes, is aware primarily of his separa-
tion from the crowd moving to and from the church and aware, too, that
the crowd is by no means a genuine community. He is the outsider, at
one with the people only by virtue of his imagination, and he shares the
"moral loneliness" which, "on week days, broods round about [the
steeple's] stately height" when the church is neglected. Thus the sketch
hints that insofar as the church is the embodiment of the institutional
center of community life, it is a failing center. "Sunday at Home" is
not one of Hawthorne's finer pieces—like a number of his other tales
and sketches, it is, as Hyatt Waggoner has said, "more interesting as a
piece of self-revelation than as a work of art"—but its juxtaposition
with "The Gray Champion" does serve to dramatize a number of those
polarities of form and meaning which are the mark of Hawthorne's art:
tale and sketch, past and present, sunshine and shadow, action and
perception, spectacle and observer, reality and illusion, community and
isolation, withdrawal and return, the innocent pleasures and the darker
pilgrimages of the imagination. The effect of this sequence is that the
implications of each piece recall and reflect those of the other. And the
effect of this interpenetration of opposites is strong enough that, together with all the other evidence, it argues for a conscious design on
Hawthorne's part.

Having eased his readers back into a familiar, prosaic—but by no
means insignificant—scene in his sketch, Hawthorne next delivers them
to a realm of Gothic melodrama in "The Wedding-Knell." There is
again a lively contrast between these two pieces, but there is also a
continuity achieved by virtue of the tale's setting. "There is a certain
church in the city of New York," Hawthorne's narrator begins, "which

I have always regarded with peculiar interest, on account of a marriage there solemnized, under very singular circumstances, in my grandmother's girlhood.'' From the reassuring conventionality of the scene in the sketch—''O, but the church is the symbol of religion,'' the non-church-going narrator concludes—we move away in space and time to a church of another stripe, a church in which is celebrated the grim wedding-funeral ceremony of Mrs. Dabney and Mr. Ellenwood. However grotesque, the story is reliable, Hawthorne again quietly assures his readers, because ''That venerable lady [the narrator's grandmother] chanced to be a spectator of the scene, and ever after made it her favorite narrative.'' The next three tales—''The Minister's Black Veil,'' ''The May-Pole of Merry Mount,'' and ''The Gentle Boy''—are among the finest in the volume, and they provide further variations on the setting of churches and religious ceremonies. They likewise move still further away from the familiar and into the past and represent the one sustained excursion Hawthorne makes into the darker, more complex and disturbing historical materials announced in ''The Gray Champion.''[2] Hawthorne's eagerness to prepare his readers is once more pronounced in his head-notes to ''The Minister's Black Veil'' and ''The May-Pole of Merry Mount,'' which, like the ruse of the narrator's grandmother, are designed to ease their journey from fact to fiction. It seems plausible, judging from his remarks about ''The Gentle Boy,'' that Hawthorne arranged these tales so as to reflect what he took to be their increasing complexity. In 1839, when publishing a separate edition of that tale, he referred to its ''imperfect and ill-wrought conception'' but concluded that ''Nature here led him deeper into the Universal Heart, than Art could follow. It was no gift within himself—no effort that could be renewed at pleasure—but a Happiness that alighted on his pen, and lent it somewhat of power over human sympathies, which he may vainly strive to catch again.''

After this group of historical tales, Hawthorne inserts ''Mr. Higginbotham's Catastrophe,'' a lengthy humorous folk tale which serves well the obvious function of providing comic relief after the demanding seriousness and moral gloom of the previous tales. The tale also investigates, if in comic terms, the tenuous relationship between, and curious interpenetration of, rumor, fantasy, and fact, imaginative

[2]Some of the reasons Hawthorne selected these historical tales rather than others are not far to seek: they were the only ones to have attracted the notice of reviewers, and such affirmation undoubtedly encouraged the unknown writer. That he also thought highly of ''The Gray Champion'' and ''The Gentle Boy'' is reflected in his use of those titles as signatures to identify eleven of his otherwise anonymous magazine stories. He never used ''Molineux,'' ''Young Goodman Brown,'' or any of the other historical tales that way.

and real experience. The mood of levity is maintained in the next piece, "Little Annie's Ramble," which, as the one sentimental juvenile sketch Hawthorne included, would seem to be related to nothing else in the volume. But preceding as it does the story of the curious vagaries of Wakefield, the account of Annie's "wandering a little way into the world" with the narrator and then returning to her mother "at the first summons, with an untainted and unwearied heart . . . [to] be a happy child again" is clearly one way Hawthorne might try simultaneously to make his fiction safe for popular taste and prepare that same taste to savor the meaning of Wakefield as "the Outcast of the Universe." The fact that the narrator himself knows that, unlike the child, he has "gone too far for the town crier to call [him] back" provides another, thematic link between the two pieces, anticipating as it does the implications of Wakefield's twenty-year absence from home and hearth.

"Wakefield" and the comic sketch, "A Rill from the Town-Pump," which follows it, are at the center of the book. Taken together, they offer an emphatic restatement of some of Hawthorne's most persistent themes, especially the patterns of withdrawal and return, alienation and community. The town pump, "as guardian of the best treasures that the town has," is the source of abiding communal life, whereas Wakefield has risked losing his place forever at the family hearth. Just as Wakefield has erred by stepping outside time altogether, so the town pump lives through generations as a symbol of permanence within history. Hawthorne, elaborating these two opposing ideas separately and sequentially here, next treats versions of them together in the following allegorical tale, "The Great Carbuncle." The central irony of the story is that, of those seeking the gem, only Hannah and Matthew finally affirm and understand the realm of the absolute; by rejecting their initial urge to possess the carbuncle, they thus reaffirm the simple values of common nature and humanity. Surely Hawthorne meant to mirror the same sort of polar opposition in placing "The Prophetic Pictures" and "David Swan" side by side. In these two stories he had turned over the same dark idea about the nature of experience and developed it in two strikingly different ways. The idea that is "illustrated by a page from the secret history of David Swan," namely, that "We can be but partially acquainted even with the events which actually influence our course through life, and our final destiny," flatly contradicts the meaning of the prophetic insights of the painter of portraits. The two pieces at once clarify and complicate one another, and their juxtaposition enriches the implications of each regarding the relationship between fiction and actuality, a motif running throughout the volume.

Immediately following the story of David Swan, a created fictional character totally unaware of "the strange things that almost happen" to him, is "Sights from a Steeple," a sketch in which Hawthorne dramatically inverts the situation in the tale and examines the same problem from the point of view, not of the character himself, but of the potentially creating artist who feels isolated from those very characters he would write about. "The most desirable mode of existence," he muses, "might be that of a spiritualized Paul Pry, hovering invisible round man and woman, witnessing their deeds, searching into their hearts, borrowing brightness from their felicity and shade from their sorrow, and retaining no emotion peculiar to himself." High aloft in his steeple perch, he yearns for creative powers reminiscent of those of the prophetic painter. And he knows he lacks such transforming insight: "But none of these things are possible; and if I would know the interior of brick walls, or the mystery of human bosoms, I can but guess." Read collectively, the three pieces have an aggregate interest which deepens their individual force. They reflect a dialectical and cumulative process.

So too do three of the last four tales—"The Hollow of the Three Hills," "The Vision of the Fountain," and "Fancy's Show-Box."[3] Each of these presents a radically "visionary" experience, and what Seymour Gross calls the "incredible sentimentality which saturates ['The Vision of the Fountain']" is set off in sharp relief by the gloom and guilt which inform the other two tales. Again there is a consciously contrived variation on similar settings in the first two of these tales. In the spot where the old crone conjures up the grim remembrances of the lady's past, "Three little hills stood near each other, and down in the midst of them sunk a hollow basin, almost mathematically circular, two or three hundred feet in breadth, and of such depth that a stately cedar might but just be visible above the sides." The spring into which, at fifteen, the love-struck narrator of the other story had gazed, "filled a circular basin, small but deep, and set round with stones, some of which were covered with slimy moss, the others naked, and of variegated hue, reddish, white, and brown." The most obviously Hawthornesque element in these settings is, of course, the perfect symmetry by which setting is symbolized as a special mode of perception. Like Mr. Smith's wine glass in "Fancy's Show-Box," they are examples of Hawthorne's use of reflecting surfaces to mirror imaginative experience. Whereas the

---

[3]Such was the order of the pieces in the 1837 volume. In 1842 "The Toll-Gatherer's Day" was inserted between the first two of these, probably for purposes of making the two volumes of equal length. Although the formal dialectical pattern was thus interrupted, the cumulative force of the group was not seriously diminished. The leading concerns of "The Toll-Gatherer's Day" are not out of place there.

vision of the first tale leads to a mysterious black baptism of knowledge and finally death for the lady and a grisly "sweet hour's sport" for the old witch, the vision of the bubbly fountain gushes forth into daylight and evaporates into the thin air of conventionality: what the young boy had imagined to be a water nymph turns out to be nothing more than "Rachel . . . the daughter of the village squire, [who] had left home for a boarding-school, the morning after [the boy] arrived and returned the day before [his] departure." The narrator concludes by dispatching all mystery. This young girl he had "transformed . . . to an angel," and he addresses a particularized audience in his last sentence: "But slight the change, sweet maids, to make angels of yourselves!" This tale was originally written as part of "The Story Teller," and, as Gross argues, when it appeared in the *New-England Magazine* (August, 1835), "it had lost its frame, and consequently its irony. We do not see a 'wayward and fanciful' youth who suffers, as he himself confesses, from 'an incorrigible levity of spirit,' . . . standing before a group of gift-book nurtured females and telling them a tale which deliberately tries to out-gift-book the gift books; we see only an incredibly bad tale." But is that all we see when we read the tale in its context in the collection? That context is one by which Hawthorne might invite even "gift-book nurtured females" to consider the value and power of the sentiments in this tale in relation to the sharply contrasting ones in the tales fore and aft. Those tales seem to me to represent Hawthorne's deliberate effort to create an ambience that would do much of the essential work of the discarded framework of "The Story Teller."

Given the diffusive dreaminess of "The Vision of the Fountain," the first words of "Fancy's Show-Box" have an undeniable rhetorical bluntness that seems calculated to jolt the lulled reader: "What is Guilt? A stain upon the soul." The reader is asked to meditate on an illustration of "the subject by an imaginary example." Mr. Smith, a venerable gentleman, has his visions, too, visions that come to him "through the brilliant medium of his glass of old Madeira" and call up the ghostly guilts of his past. Whereas there is no question of the lady's guilt in "The Hollow of the Three Hills" and no question of the youth's untried innocence in "The Vision of the Fountain," "Fancy's Show-Box" takes up in the most straightforward allegorical terms the problematic nature of guilt and innocence in human behavior and in so doing encompasses the materials and attitudes of the other two tales. Hawthorne ends the story by asking the reader to join him in formulating a defense of Mr. Smith and argues the man's innocence on the grounds that "It is not until the crime is accomplished that guilt clinches its gripe upon the guilty heart, and claims it for its own." Yet, he warns, "Man must not disclaim his brotherhood, even with the guiltiest, since, though his hand be clean, his heart has surely been polluted by the flitting phantoms of iniquity.'' Neither man nor the ''sweet maids'' for whom ''The Vision of the Fountain'' was especially intended, dare neglect their membership in that universal brotherhood of sin and guilt. Clearly Hawthorne's ploy has been to lead his genteel readers on to an acceptance of the somber moral outlook of ''Fancy's Show-Box'' after first allowing them to indulge their sentimental superficiality in the story of youthful love.

To view *Twice-Told Tales* as a series of disconnected fragments is to be able to say that ''The Vision of the Fountain'' would have meant the same thing had it been placed anywhere in the volume—say, opening the collection and followed by ''The Gray Champion'' or sandwiched between ''A Rill from the Town-Pump'' and ''Sights from the Steeple'' at the end of the book. While such sequences as these are obviously meaningless, there are undoubtedly other possible combinations capable of eliciting coherent patterns of some kind. My point is simply that the collection as it stands is not a haphazard gathering and that the arrangement of tales and sketches bespeaks Hawthorne's conscious dialectical design.

''Fancy's Show-Box'' at once presents a synthesis for the polarities formed by ''The Hollow of the Three Hills'' and ''The Vision of the Fountain'' and provides another purposeful dramatic contrast to ''Dr. Heidegger's Experiment,'' the final tale in the volume. Whereas Mr. Smith's glass of Madeira operates as an efficacious sign of the transforming imagination and leads to genuine moral insights, the powers of the elixir that Dr. Heidegger offers in champagne glasses to his aged guests are as illusory and unsubstantial as the boy's vision of the angelic girl. Worse than that, they are also dangerous and destructive for the four old fools who, suffering from the delusion that they can recapture their lost youth and innocence, are induced to make a pilgrimage to Florida. Hawthorne ends the collection, then, with a tale which evaluates once again the dangers of abusing the possibilities of imaginative experience by seeking in them an escape from the conditions of the real world. He ends it, too, with a tale that registers in the cool detachment of the necromancer-artist Heidegger (whose attitude contrasts markedly with that of Hawthorne in ''Fancy's Show-Box'') the complicity Hawthorne felt the artist himself shares in titillating an audience with spurious and irresponsible imaginative forms.

Having begun the collection with a tale projecting a strong sense of community and the pledge that ''New England's sons will vindicate their ancestry,'' he concludes it centrifugally, with a manipulative artist-figure and his audience, mere objects of his icy experimentation, isolated in a world of effervescent illusion. Implicit in the last tale is Hawthorne's insistence that fiction, having led the reader through the "kingdom of possibilities," should return him once again to the world of actuality. The return to actuality is one of the foremost functions of the meditative and descriptive sketches—"Sunday at Home," "A Rill from the Town-Pump," "Sights from a Steeple"—which act as interludes and, like the heavily pointed sentences, slow the pace and turn the reader inward to a thoughtful consideration of the meaning of imaginative experience.

The 1837 volume is one in which Hawthorne deliberately included something for everyone—children, delicate ladies, hardheaded businessmen. He was determined to write for his own age as well as for posterity and so, despite all his disclaimers, he tried, as he once remarked, "to extend and vary his audience as much as possible" in order to validate what was for him a full and healthy range of sensibilities. His alterations of "The Vision of the Fountain" suggest that, in deleting passages that parodied his readers' favorite gift-book form, he subdued what must have been at times a strong urge to satirize the sentimental bent of his audience. Instead, his basic strategy was to minister to rather than exploit the needs of the wide audience he was always hoping to attract. Like Irving, he turned his impulse toward parody and satire in upon himself, and the result was his creation, most noticeable in the sketches, of a variety of narrative voices: now doubtful and timid, now assertive, but always modulated by a characteristic irony. Including something for everyone, he did not set his pieces *in vacuo*. Attempting to satisfy simultaneously the demands of his audience and the demands of his art, he so arranged his tales and sketches that they would mediate between one another. The device of the "procession," which informs many individual pieces, Hawthorne used also as a structural principle binding the tales collectively. He wished to take his readers by the hand, without their knowing it, and to lead them through the realm of his imagination. Thus did he confront what Terence Martin says Hawthorne saw as his "essential problem": "To create not simply fiction but the conditions of fiction." The arrangement of the collection as a whole likewise epitomizes the "bifurcated Hawthorne," the artist with his dedication to the imaginative order and the man of the world who sympathizes with and actively shares his audience's demands for actuality. The sequence of tales in 1837 reflects Hawthorne's energetic control over these two impulses and his careful balancing of their polarizing claims.

Marshall Van Deusen

Narrative Tone in "The Custom House" and The Scarlet Letter

Almost as though they wished to make common cause with Hawthorne's outraged fellow-townsmen of Salem, twentieth-century critics have pretty consistently seen "The Custom House" as an inappropriate introduction to *The Scarlet Letter,* trivial in matter and unworthy in manner; and thus they have shrugged it off as irrelevant to the "masterpiece" which follows it. Hawthorne's own explanations to his publisher of his reasons for including "The Custom House" (that his book needed to be made fatter and the gloom lightened) have not encouraged later critics to a serious examination of the relationship between the introduction and the romance proper. Yet "The Custom House" does comprise about one sixth the total length of *The Scarlet Letter,* and it does, as Hawthorne and his critics agree, complicate the tone of the whole book. Perhaps some examination of the narrative voice in "The Custom House" and its echoes in the romance that follows (for it seems to me that it does echo throughout the book) may serve to clarify the matter of the adjustment, or maladjustment, of tones between the two parts, and so suggest how the parts go together to make one whole. Such an examination may even make Hawthorne's allegorical method, which Henry James was so skeptical of, seem rather more "modern," even more "dramatic" in a Jamesian sense of the term, than we have heretofore thought—though perhaps a "revaluation" of quite that degree of irony is not wholly to be wished.

From Nineteenth-Century Fiction, *Vol. 21, No. 1, June 1966, pp. 61–71, by permission of The Regents. Copyright © by The Regents of the University of California.*

Edward Wagenknecht's remarks (in *Cavalcade of the American Novel*, New York, 1952) provide a convenient way of coming quickly to the point which I think has been so consistently missed. After deploring the "casualness" of tone which makes the introduction "hopelessly out of harmony" with the romance proper, Wagenknecht flatly concludes that "The Custom House" has "no real connection with the story of *The Scarlet Letter*." The failure of connection is proved by Hawthorne's "pretending à la Defoe that he found Hester's story in some old papers at the Custom House"; for Wagenknecht, it is clearly "too late in the day for anything like that to be either necessary or convincing." However it was with Defoe, it seems perfectly clear that with Hawthorne the discovery of those papers *is* a pretense, and that the wry, quizzical irony of the pretense sets a tonal pattern which introduces, and in large measure defines, the problems of knowledge, historical and relative, real and absolute, which are such an important part of the thematic material of the book.

Austin Warren, in his "Introduction" to the Rinehart edition of *The Scarlet Letter* (New York, 1947), unwittingly confirms this way of understanding Hawthorne's "pretending." He writes:

> A traditional device of novelists is to offer a fiction as a true story, a document. Thus Hawthorne professes to have discovered, among old papers at the Custom House, "half a dozen sheets of foolscap" summarizing the life of Hester Prynne, together with the actual scarlet letter she wore; and further to dispel all doubt, he specifies with the realistic precision of Defoe and Swift, that each arm of the letter is "precisely three inches and a quarter in length."

Warren explains, however, that "there is not the slightest reason for crediting this discovery," because Hawthorne had, in 1837, already made use of the idea of Hester's punishment in "Endicott and the Red Cross." Warren insists, therefore, that *"The Scarlet Letter* is a romance, not a chronicle." But surely there is no question of crediting literally Hawthorne's story about his discovery of the faded scarlet letter and the manuscript of "Mr. Surveyor Pue." "The Custom House" makes such a mistake less likely rather than more so, for Hawthorne explicitly tells us that even "The life of the Custom House lies like a dream behind me," and he has nicely calculated his tone in those "realistic" details about the measurement of the letter as a way of debunking the narrowness and irrelevance of the solemn documentarians, and as a way of marking a whole range of problems concerning the nature of knowledge and evidence.[1] Rather than dispelling "all doubt," the mixture of fact and fancy in his account of his employment at the Custom House, and the mixture of present and past in the reflections it stimulates, are the beginning of Hawthorne's exploration of that "neutral territory, somewhere between the real world and fairy-land, where the Actual and the Imaginary may meet"; that exploration is continued among the gloomy shadows and flickering lights of Hester's and Dimmesdale's trial of doubt and faith, a trial which is complicated for the "liberated" nineteenth-century functionary of the Republic by being an aspect of a seventeenth-century society that at every point challenges his own moral and historical (one might almost say his anthropological) imagination.

The mood of romance is set in "The Custom House," and it is not set simply by the famous passage there about moonlight. It is felt throughout the preface, and perhaps especially in the paragraphs that include the mention of those curiously circumstantial measurements of the scarlet letter. Those details, in context, are not in the service of literary verisimilitude but of a symbolic ambiguity which centers for the moment on the problem of the meaning of historical authenticity. "The Ancient Surveyor" seems to have been "a local antiquarian"; yet some of "his facts" have found their way into Hawthorne's fictionalized article on "Main Street." Hawthorne's ironic tone is surely unmistakable when he remarks that "as a final disposition" of the "remainder" of Pue's facts, "I contemplate depositing them with the Essex Historical Society." And his pun is surely intended when he contends that "the main facts" of *The Scarlet Letter* "are *authorized* (my italics) and authenticated by the document of Mr. Surveyor Pue," for two sentences later he admits that in some places "I have allowed myself . . . nearly or altogether as much license as if the facts had been entirely of my own invention."

Nearly or altogether! In the second paragraph of his preface Hawthorne had introduced the ironic note by claiming to offer "proofs of the authenticity of (his) narrative" and claiming for himself only "my true position as editor, or very little more." Solemnly he asserted that "this and no other is my true reason for assuming a personal

---

[1]The example of Washington Irving is the most obvious reminder that the "historical" documentation of fictional narratives and tales was a commom enough convention in Hawthorne's literary environment. But a thorough study of Hawthorne's sense of history in its literary and general epistemological bearings would be of great value to students of his mind and art and to students of American intellectual history as well.

relation with the public''! He wished to offer his ''proofs'' and to justify the ''few extra touches'' he had allowed himself.

Now, thirty pages later, it turns out that all Hawthorne contends for ''is the authenticity of the outline''! The story of the scarlet letter is his story, not Mr. Surveyor Pue's. For, ''I must not be understood,'' he writes, ''as affirming, that, in the dressing up of the tale, and imagining the motives and modes of passion that influenced the characters who figure in it, I have invariably confined myself within the limits of the old Surveyor's half a dozen sheets of foolscap.'' It also develops that these sheets of foolscap ''were documents . . . not official, but of a private nature,'' even though Jonathan Pue had been a historian. And Hawthorne's own name, imprinted ''with a stencil and black paint, on pepper bags, and baskets of anatto, and cigar-boxes, and bales of all kinds of dutiable merchandise,'' had authorized and authenticated official governmental acts, though he was a writer of romances. Finally, by a kind of ironic *dédoublement* of perspective Hawthorne speculates that his fictional writings rather than his official acts may perhaps become ''materials of local history.''

Hawthorne's tone in these remarks—and its manifold variations throughout the preface—is important. He is mocking the easy belief that a historian can penetrate truth by a simple disposition of his little hoard of ''facts.'' But in these passages—and throughout the preface, especially in his account of his responses to his dismissal from the Custom House—he is also mocking himself; and in the ironic intensity of his hypnotic fascination with the letter itself, as well as in the long passage which culminates in his vision of fire and moonlight within the ''haunted verge'' of the looking glass, he is even mocking his mockery. ''The Custom House'' reflects not simply the wit and urbanity of the accomplished essayist; rather the urbanity exists to qualify and ameliorate the haunting and otherwise haunted reflections of the imaginative amateur of epistemology. The complication of tones defines more than doubt; it defines also a person; and that person is, by his own admission, the narrator of the whole *Scarlet Letter,* as well as of ''The Custom House''; he is everywhere present in the whole book; it is his voice that interprets (creates?) Hester's and Dimmesdale's story. It is in this sense that the tone of ''The Custom House'' begins to define the content of *The Scarlet Letter.* In this sense Hawthorne, or more properly, the Surveyor of Customs who was also a sometime writer of tales and sketches and who is now the ''editor'' of a historical romance, is a character in that romance, and his voice, with its complication of tones echoes throughout the book. Not to know the Surveyor is, thus, to miss some of the thematic concerns (*his* concerns) of *The Scarlet Letter* and to miss the characteristic interpretation which his voice gives them as he explores and tests their implications.

A few critics have noted thematic "parallels" between "The Custom House" and the rest of *The Scarlet Letter*. Among these critics Sam S. Baskett [in *"The (Complete) Scarlet Letter," College English,* XXII (Feb., 1961), 321–328] has given the best account of the thematic interrelations between the two parts of the whole romance. He calls attention to the contrast between the decay of the somnolent society of nineteenth-century Salem and the iron vigor and strength of the sterner society of seventeenth-century Boston. He points out how the new society is characterized by shallow commercialism and petty politics as opposed to the characteristically religious and moral concerns which ordered the life of Puritan New England. The easy, shuffling tolerance of latter-day liberalism (whether materialistic or transcendental) is no better than the harsh dogmatism of the Puritan community, for in the "later community judgment and punishment are awarded capriciously, chaotically, without reference to an ultimate framework." In the "fragmented" secular world of the nineteenth century, genuine ethical concerns have disappeared in a welter of expediency and improvisation. And the men of new Salem are pathetic heirs of the men of old Boston. The Inspector thinks principally of his stomach; the man of business is primarily concerned with the figures in his account book; and the old soldier, who retains faint memories of his own days of heroism, in which physical courage and moral duty were at least nominally united, is, after all, a childish anachronism in the new bureaucracy.

Baskett goes on to explain that even more important in "The Custom House" than "the external ironic contrast" between two societies is the problem of "the relation of the individual to whatever the society, irrespective of its nature, in which he finds himself." Hawthorne's problem as an alienated artist who, nevertheless, regrets his alienation and hopes that he may yet participate in the "United effort of mankind" is certainly similar to Hester's problem, and to Chillingworth's, and to Dimmesdale's: it is the problem of the outsider's need to negotiate without bitterness with the real but imperfect world around him, and it is the problem also of orthodoxy's need to recognize the imperfection of its own generalized demands in the face of individual cases. Perhaps the *hubris* of the individual and the *hubris* of society must both bow before an ultimate mystery.

To list the thematic parallels between "The Custom House" and the romance that follows it is not, however, to demonstrate its "appropriateness" as a preface. Hawthorne's themes are notoriously recurrent throughout all his work. The theme of mediating between individual conscience and social orthodoxy is a central theme in "The Gentle Boy" and, with some variations, in "The Maypole of Merrymount" and "The Artist of the Beautiful," to cite only three obvious examples. In fact, a preoccupation with problems of alienation is perhaps the single most pervasive thematic characteristic of Hawthorne's work from "Rappaccini's Daughter" and "Ethan Brand" to *The Blithedale Romance* and the late unfinished works. The list of "representative connections between 'The Custom House' and *The Scarlet Letter*" might, as Baskett says, "be considerably lengthened." My own very brief description of some of these connections is partly a paraphrase of Baskett's list and partly a suggestion for its extension. But by the same token, and quite as easily, we might also lengthen very considerably the list of other works which share in this network of connections. And to do this would not be relevant to the question raised by other critics concerning the suitability of "The Custom House" as an introduction to *The Scarlet Letter*. This is a problem which the listing of thematic parallels largely ignores.

The "Custom House" does more than introduce themes to be developed in the romance that follows. As I have suggested, it introduces also the character and voice of the narrator, that is of the "decapitated surveyor." And it is the echoing of that voice, sometimes querulous, sometimes self-doubting, throughout *The Scarlet Letter* that binds the two parts of the book into an indissoluble whole. We may notice, for example, that "the external ironic contrast" Baskett mentions between seventeenth- and nineteenth-century New England society becomes quite characteristically internal for Hawthorne in his praise and accusation of his ancestors (their "dim and dusky grandeur" coexisting with their "persecuting spirit") and in his defense and accusation of their descendant ("an idler like myself" who is a "writer of story books!"). This contrast at least is a matter of personal tension that serves to characterize the narrator as well as the societies of which he speaks. And it is this personal tension that "explains" and prepares us for the notorious doubleness of judgment which pervades the story of Hester's persecution.

The doubleness is enforced upon our attention very early in that story. Hester is characterized at the outset as possessed of "natural dignity," but she is also "haughty" and displays "a desperate recklessness of . . . mood." And there is a curious mixture of ironic diffidence and plaintive wishfulness in the narrator's quasi-blasphemous "Papist" comparison of her appearance to "the image of Divine Maternity, . . . whose infant was to redeem the world." And what of Hester's judges? In the first scene the narrator speaks with the enlightened assurance of the nineteenth-century progressive of "the whole dismal severity of the Puritanic code of law"; but he speaks also as the historical relativist in noting a "solemnity of demeanor on the part of the spectators" which "befitted a people amongst whom religion and law were almost identical, and in whose character both were so thoroughly interfused, that the mildest and severest acts of public discipline were alike made venerable and awful." And finally the personal reminiscence of his own experience in the Custom House surely lies behind his judgment that "The scene (before the jail) was not without a mixture of awe, such as must always invest the spectacle of guilt and shame in a fellow-creature, before society shall have grown corrupt enough to smile, instead of shuddering, at it." For despite the stern severity of Hester's judges, there was in them "none of the heartlessness of another social state, which would find only a theme of jest in an exhibition like the present."

I have suggested that in "The Custom House" Hawthorne, through his dramatic representation of himself, confronts the problem of historical knowledge, and by clear implication more general epistemological problems. In the first few pages of the romance proper he reminds us insistently and, if we remember his voice in "The Custom House," characteristically, that Hester Prynne's story is itself a historical problem that involves at once an understanding of *autre temps, autre moeurs,* and a recognition of persistent patterns of human behavior. "The founders," he says, "of a new colony, whatever Utopia of human virtue and happiness they might originally project, have invariably recognized it among their earliest practical necessities to allot a portion of the virgin soil as a cemetery, and another portion as the site of a prison." And although the Puritan New England colony is, Hawthorne recalls, in its infancy, the door of the jail to which our attention is fixed on the very first page of the historical narrative, seems "Like all that pertains to crime . . . never to have known a youthful era." As for the rose bush, we cannot say whether it is rumor and legend or historical fact that connects it with "the sainted Anne Hutchinson." But "It may serve, let us hope, to symbolize some sweet moral blossom, that may be found along the track, or relieve the darkening close of a tale of human frailty and sorrow." That "let us hope," taken together with the defensive humor of the narrator's remarks about death and crime, is a way of combining the moralistic optimism of the nineteenth-century civil servant with the ironic skepticism of the sometime author of romances whose experience in the real world has made him unsure of that world and also of himself. We hear, thus, the echo of a voice as much as the echo of a theme. We hear perhaps the dramatic definition of a theme, and thus we understand its complexity in a way we could not were it presented "straight."

In these opening pages of Hester's story Hawthorne, the historical editor, even permits himself some of the same sort of musing digressions practiced in the preface by Hawthorne, the informal essayist. He describes the "not unsubstantial persons" of the women in the crowd by the prison door with their "broad shoulders and well-developed busts . . . and round and ruddy cheeks, that had ripened in the far-off island (England), and had hardly yet grown paler or thinner in the atmosphere of New England." In the best manner of the informal essayist, he wryly spins out his genetic explanation: "Morally, as well as materially, there was a coarser fibre in those wives and maidens of old English birth and breeding, than in their fair descendants, separated from them by a series of six or seven generations; for, throughout that chain of ancestry, every successive mother has transmitted to her child a fainter bloom, a more delicate and briefer beauty, and a slighter physical frame, if not a character of less force and solidity, than her own." Such a digression reminds us not simply of the contrast between two ages, for that contrast is hardly very objective, nor is it meant to be. We hear instead the voice of a particular narrator, speaking from the de-feminized, yet vaguely effeminate, world of the Custom House, offering a very proper, yet strangely envious, criticism of the decidedly female, yet curiously masculine, women of his imagination. We hear a voice that plays urbanely with paradox as the only instrument adequate for controlling its own doubts, and which is yet a means of releasing them and giving them a dangerous license. We recognize the voice because we have met the speaker in "The Custom House."

Without such a recognition early in the game (for this romance is a kind of game, albeit a very serious one), we are likely to misestimate the import of many of the auctorial comments at crucial points. One passage will perhaps suffice to indicate what I mean. When Dimmesdale is returning home from the crucial interview with Hester (and Pearl) in the forest, he feels a strong urge to blaspheme and to address the most shocking crudities and impurities to the people he meets on the way. The narrator comments:

> Tempted by a dream of happiness, he had yielded himself with deliberate choice, as he had never done before, to what he knew was deadly sin. And the infectious poison of that sin had been thus rapidly diffused throughout his moral system. It had stupefied all blessed impulses, and awakened into vivid life the whole brotherhood of bad ones.

Ernest Sandeen has cited this passage in his persuasive article on *"The Scarlet Letter* as a Love Story" [*PMLA,* LXXVII (Sept., 1962), 425–435] and has rightly sensed the importance of its tone. The tone, he says, is one of "solemn moralism" and "pious pontificating," which Hawthorne "has made a part of (the narrator's) character." But Sandeen nowhere identifies the narrator, nor does he really seem to have any genuine sense of his "character," certainly not of him *as* a character. In another reference to a tone of "gloomy moralistic exaggeration," he speaks simply of Hawthorne's "narrative voice," and he suggests that "most, if not all," of the narrator's sermonizings are "Hawthorne's concession to his reader's prejudices"; yet he insists that "they serve simultaneously to keep clearly in view the moral distinctions which form the basic structure of the novel." Apparently they can be used in this way because the concession is ironic: "Some of the pious lectures which this narrative voice delivers are so plainly out of key with what is going on that we may suspect they are pieces of calculated irony." But Sandeen is uneasy with such an explanation and seems finally to wish to evade the problem by noting simply that the "tone of the narrative comments" sometimes runs "against the grain" and sometimes "with the grain of the narrative context."

Sandeen's sensitiveness to tone seems to me to invite such questions as, "Whose tone?" and "Why is there a special 'narrative voice' at all?" The failure to identify the narrator not only leaves him a rather puzzling technical complication, but also leaves the tone of such a passage as the one cited a kind of simple, unconscious irony which the reader and, presumably, Hawthorne too see through from a superior vantage point of amused condescension. Thus, the religious and ethical perspectives urged by the narrator's vocabulary are reduced in seriousness and *The Scarlet Letter* tends to be simplified into an "attack" on outmoded ideas from the point of view of progressive, enlightened liberalism. Such a result is clearly far from Sandeen's intention, and certainly it is false to the pervasive ambivalence of attitude which persists throughout the story of Hester's "persecution" and Dimmesdale's "salvation." But to forget the narrator we have met in the Custom House makes it difficult to understand and account for the complexity of perspective which Sandeen himself seems to feel in the development of the narrative proper, and difficult to understand and account for the variety of tones which we have heard this unsimple voice encompass at the very outset of that narrative.

To hear only or principally a tone of unconscious irony in the narrative of *The Scarlet Letter* suggests that the narrator, whoever he is, is a kind of fool, a figure of fun, whose viewpoint is simply rejected, and who is from our superior viewpoint not a part of the issues he bumblingly describes. He becomes a figure outside the drama, at best a mild kind of comic relief. But if we think of him as integrally related to the narrative through the Hawthorne of the preface, the historical, epistemological, and ethical themes of the whole book will be recognized as more serious and more subtle by virtue of their dramatic relationship to a character of genuinely complex intelligence and delicate sensibility. Even if we should imagine that in some passages we are hearing the voice, not of the "decapitated surveyor," but of "Mr. Surveyor Pue," we are taken back to the Custom House and we remember that Hawthorne has as much admiration as condescension for that worthy. We cannot be condescending even toward *his* voice. The "moralism" in *The Scarlet Letter* is not simple-minded; it is part of a range of tones of considerable variety, and though it may occasionally sound plaintive or nostalgic, there is an appeal in its winning simplicity that is almost as compelling as our sense of its final inadequacy. If we remember the sophisticated doubts about sophistication expressed by the author of the preface, the naive tone of parts of the narrative proper may be seen as part of a dramatic testing of attitudes which defines a central epistemological issue that qualifies our understanding of all the themes of the book. In this sense, if in no other, "The Custom House" and our acquaintance with the mind and sensibility of its central character are an essential and indispensable part of our experience of *The Scarlet Letter*.

Hawthorne's careful management of narrative tone and his use of a carefully controlled narrative voice as an aspect of general narrative technique deserve to be studied in the romances that followed *The Scarlet Letter*, and indeed in the tales and sketches that preceded it. Hawthorne has said on the opening page of "The Custom House" that "thoughts are frozen and utterance benumbed, unless the speaker stand in some true relation with his audience." In his most considerable published work before *The Scarlet Letter*, he had sensed the possibilities for establishing such a relationship in a literary convention that lay ready at hand, the convention that Washington Irving had so charmingly popularized in "The Author's Account of Himself" prefaced to *The Sketch Book*. In "The Old Manse" Hawthorne's experiments with this convention had shown its great possibilities as a means of anticipating the themes and qualifying the spirit and tone of the *Tales* that followed. In "The Custom House," through the full exploitation of these possibilities and through the establishment of a dramatic "personal relation" between the author and his narrative, as well as between the author and his audience, he raised the convention to high art.

Richard Harter Fogle

The Poetics of Concealment: The Scarlet Letter

Interpretations of *The Scarlet Letter* have been almost startlingly various. This is not surprising, for Hawthorne has himself pointed the way to a wide range of speculations. The concluding words of *The Scarlet Letter,* however, summarily dismiss the more cheerful readings, of which there are a number. In describing the heraldic device on the common tombstone of Hester and Dimmesdale, they describe "our now concluded legend; so sombre is it, and relieved only by one ever-glowing point of light gloomier than the shadow:—

'On a Field, Sable, the Letter A, Gules.' "

These words alone, in my opinion, are sufficient evidence for disproving the notion that *The Scarlet Letter* is "about" Hester Prynne the advanced feminist, or that the story can be satisfactorily summarized either by the moral which Hawthorne attaches to Dimmesdale, " 'Show freely to the world, if not your worst, yet some trait whereby the worst may be inferred!' ' 'or by the doctrine of *felix culpa,* "the fortunate fall," that out of sin and evil comes good and that Hester is educated and refined by her wrongdoing. The sentiment is too darkly tragic to be appropriate to any of these conclusions, though Hawthorne at one place and another in *The Scarlet Letter* has suggested the possibility of all of them. The true conclusion of *The Scarlet Letter* is an unresolved contradiction—unresolved not from indecision or lack of thought but from honesty of imagination. Hawthorne gives the only answer that his formulation of the terms permits. If we consider that the problem of *The Scarlet Letter* is primarily the problem of Hester Prynne, the verdict is

From Hawthorne's Fiction: The Light and the Dark *by Richard Harter Fogle (rev. ed., 1964). Copyright © 1952, 1964 by the University of Oklahoma Press. Reprinted by permission of the author and that of the University of Oklahoma Press.*

at best suspension of judgment after full examination of the evidence. And, as we know, Hester emerges from trial in better condition than her codefendants Dimmesdale and Chillingworth.

This is the contradiction, and a very widely representative contradiction it is: the sin of *The Scarlet Letter* is a symbol of the original sin, by which no man is untouched. All mortals commit the sin in one form or another, which is perhaps the meaning of "your worst" in the exhortation occasioned by the death of Dimmesdale. Hester, having sinned, makes the best possible recovery; and the crime itself is of all crimes the most excusable, coming of passionate love and having "a consecration of its own." Yet the sin remains real and inescapable, and she spends her life in retribution, the death of her lover Dimmesdale having finally taught her that this is the only way. This is the dilemma: human beings by their natures must fall into error—and yet it would be better if they did not.

The letter, an "ever-glowing point of light," is gloomier than the shadow of its background. The shadow, the "Field, Sable," is roughly the atmosphere of Puritanism, the "Letter A, Gules" the atmosphere of the sin. These are at odds, and no absolute superiority is granted to either. The Puritan doctors are no fit judges of a woman's heart; nor, on the other hand, is Hester to be absolved. The letter is glowing, positive, vital, the product of genuine passion, while the sable may certainly be taken as the negation of everything alive. Yet the letter is gloomier.

These shades are both of hell, and there is no hue of heaven in *The Scarlet Letter* which really offsets them. Sunlight is the nearest approach to it, and its sway is too fleeting to have any great effect. In the forest scene of chapters XVI–XIX sunshine, "as with a sudden smile of heaven," bursts over Hester and Dimmesdale, but this is merely a momentary relief. The hope which accompanies it is short-lived, delusory, and dangerous. A more steadfast light, "The sun, but little past its meridian," shines down upon Dimmesdale as he stands on the scaffold to confess his guilt. This is triumph, indeed, but little to counterbalance the continual power of the "bale fire" and "lurid gleam" of the letter. Hope and regeneration are sometimes symbolized in Hawthorne by the celestial colors of dawn, transfigured by light: blues, greens, and golds. In "Ethan Brand" the tender hues of the twilight sky are overpowered by night and the red and black of Brand's Unpardonable Sin, but they are revivified by the atmosphere of dawn. So the storm in *The House of the Seven Gables,* which accompanies the crisis and blows itself out with the death of Judge Pyncheon, gives way to a world made new and bathed in morning sunshine. There is no such scene in *The Scarlet Letter*.

The problem of *The Scarlet Letter* can be solved only by introducing the supernatural level of heaven, the sphere of absolute knowledge and justice and—hesitantly—of complete fulfillment. This may seem to be another paradox, and perhaps a disappointing one. Without doubt *The Scarlet Letter* pushes *towards* the limit of moral judgment, suggesting many possible conclusions. It is even relentless in its search in the depths of its characters. There is yet, however, a point beyond which Hawthorne will not go; ultimate solutions are not appropriate in the merely human world. His sympathy with Hester and Dimmesdale is clear enough, but he allows them only to escape the irrevocable spiritual ruin which befalls Chillingworth. Figuratively his good wishes pursue them beyond life, but he does not presume himself to absolve them. Even in the carefully staged scene of Dimmesdale's death, where every impulse of both author and reader demands complete forgiveness, Hawthorne refuses to grant it. With his "bright dying eyes" Dimmesdale looks into eternity, but nothing he sees there permits him to comfort Hester. To her questions, " 'Shall we not meet again? . . . Shall we not spend our immortal life together?' " he can answer only, " 'The law we broke!—the sin here so awfully revealed!—let these alone be in thy thoughts! I fear! I fear!' " A grim and unflinching conclusion, considering everything. Dimmesdale is not of course Hawthorne, but the very preservation of dramatic propriety at this crucial point is significant.

There are four states of being in Hawthorne: one subhuman, two human, and one superhuman. The first is Nature, which comes to our attention in *The Scarlet Letter* twice. It appears first in the opening chapter, in the wild rosebush which stands outside the blackbrowed Puritan jail, and whose blossoms

> might be imagined to offer their fragrance and fragile beauty to the prisoner as he went in, and to the condemned criminal as he came forth to his doom, in token that the deep heart of Nature could pity and be kind to him.

The second entrance of Nature comes in the forest scene, where it sympathizes with the forlorn lovers and gives them hope. "Such was the sympathy of Nature—that wild, heathen Nature of the forest, never subjugated by human law, nor illumined by higher truth. . . ." The sentence epitomizes both the virtues of Nature and its inadequacy. In itself good, Nature is not a sufficient support for human beings.

The human levels are represented by Hawthorne's distinction between Heart and Head. The heart is closer to nature, the head to the supernatural. The heart may err by lapsing into nature, which means, since it has not the innocence of nature, into corruption. The danger of the head lies in the opposite direction. It aspires to be superhuman and is likely to dehumanize itself in the attempt by violating the human limit. Dimmesdale, despite his considerable intellect, is predominantly a heart character, and it is through the heart that sin has assailed him, in a burst of passion which overpowered both religion and reason. The demoniac Chillingworth is of the head, a cold experimenter and thinker. It is fully representative of Hawthorne's general emphasis that Chillingworth's spiritual ruin is complete. Hester Prynne is a combination of head and heart, with a preponderance of head. Her original sin is of passion, but its consequences expose her to the danger of absolute mental isolation. The centrifugal urge of the intellect is counteracted in her by her duty to her daughter Pearl, the product of the sin, and by her latent love for Dimmesdale. Pearl herself is a creature of nature, most at home in the wild forest: ". . . the mother-forest, and these wild things which it nourished, all recognized a kindred wildness in the human child." She is made human by Dimmesdale's confession and death: "The great scene of grief, in which the wild infant bore a part, had developed all her sympathies. . . ."

The fourth level, the superhuman or heavenly, will perhaps merely be confused by elaborate definition. It is the sphere of absolute insight, justice, and mercy. Few of Hawthorne's tales and romances can be adequately considered without taking it into account. As Mark Van Doren has recently emphasized, it is well to remember Hawthorne's belief in immortality. It is because of the very presence of the superhuman in Hawthorne's thinking that the destinies of his chief characters are finally veiled in ambiguity. He respects them as he would have respected any real person by refusing to pass the last judgment, by leaving a residue of mysterious individuality untouched. The whole truth is not for a fellow human to declare.

These four states are not mutually exclusive. Without the touch of nature human life would be too bleak. The Puritans of *The Scarlet Letter* are deficient in nature, and they are consequently dour and over-righteous. Something of the part that nature might play in the best human life is suggested in the early chapters of *The Marble Faun*, particularly through the character Donatello. The defects of either Heart or Head in a state of isolation have already been mentioned. And without some infusion of superhuman meaning into the spheres of the human, life would be worse than bestial. Perhaps only one important character in all of Hawthorne's works finds it possible to dispense completely with heaven—Westervelt, of *The Blithedale Romance*—and he is essentially diabolic. In some respects the highest and the lowest of these levels are most closely akin, as if their relationship were as points of a circle. The innocence of nature is like the innocence of heaven. It is at times, when compared to the human, like the Garden before the serpent, like heaven free of the taint of evil. Like infancy, however, nature is a stage which man must pass through, whereas his destination is heaven. The juxtaposition of highest and lowest nevertheless involves difficulties, when perfect goodness seems equivalent to mere deprivation and virtue seems less a matter of choosing than of being untempted.

The intensity of *The Scarlet Letter,* at which Hawthorne himself was dismayed, comes from concentration, selection, and dramatic irony. The concentration upon the central theme is unremitting. The tension is lessened only once, in the scene in the forest, and then only delusively, since the hope of freedom which brings it about is quickly shown to be false and even sinful. The characters play out their tragic action against a background in itself oppressive—the somber atmosphere of Puritanism. Hawthorne calls the progression of the story "the darkening close of a tale of human frailty and sorrow." Dark to begin with, it grows steadily deeper in gloom. The method is almost unprecedentedly selective. Almost every image has a symbolic function; no scene is superfluous. One would perhaps at times welcome a loosening of the structure, a moment of wandering from the path. The weedy grassplot in front of the prison; the distorting reflection of Hester in a breastplate, where the Scarlet Letter appears gigantic; the tapestry of David and Bathsheba on the wall of the minister's chamber; the little brook in the forest; the slight malformation of Chillingworth's shoulder; the ceremonial procession on election day—in every instance more is meant than meets the eye.

The intensity of *The Scarlet Letter* comes in part from a sustained and rigorous dramatic irony, or irony of situation. This irony arises naturally from the theme of "secret sin," or concealment. "Show freely of your worst," says Hawthorne; the action of *The Scarlet Letter* arises from the failure of Dimmesdale and Chillingworth to do so. The minister hides his sin, and Chillingworth hides his identity. This concealment affords a constant drama. There is the irony of Chapter III, "The Recognition," in which Chillingworth's ignorance is suddenly and blindingly reversed. Separated from his wife by many vicissitudes, he comes upon her as she is dramatically exposed to public infamy. From his instantaneous decision, symbolized by the lifting of his finger to his lips to hide his tie to her, he precipitates the further irony of his sustained hypocrisy.

In the same chapter Hester is confronted with her fellow-adulterer, who is publicly called upon to persuade her as her spiritual guide to reveal his identity. Under the circumstances the situation is highly charged, and his words have a double meaning—one to the onlookers, another far different to Hester and the speaker himself. " 'If thou feelest it to be for thy soul's peace, and that thy earthly punishment will therefore be made more effectual to salvation, I charge thee to speak out the name of thy fellow-sinner and fellow-sufferer!' "

From this scene onward Chillingworth, by living a lie, arouses a constant irony, which is also an ambiguity. With a slight shift in emphasis all his actions can be given a very different interpretation. Seen purely from without, it would be possible to regard him as completely blameless. Hester expresses this ambiguity in Chapter IV, after he has ministered to her sick baby, the product of her faithlessness, with tenderness and skill. " 'Thy acts are like mercy,' said Hester, bewildered and appalled. 'But thy words interpret thee as a terror!' " Masquerading as a physician, he becomes to Dimmesdale a kind of attendant fiend, racking the minister's soul with constant anguish. Yet outwardly he has done him nothing but good. " 'What evil have I done the man?' asked Roger Chillingworth again. 'I tell thee, Hester Prynne, the richest fee that ever physician earned from monarch could not have bought such care as I have wasted on this miserable priest!' " Even when he closes the way to escape by proposing to take passage on the same ship with the fleeing lovers, it is possible to consider the action merely friendly. His endeavor at the end to hold Dimmesdale back from the saving scaffold is from one point of view reasonable and friendlike, although he is a devil struggling to snatch back an escaping soul. " 'All shall be well! Do not blacken your fame, and perish in dishonor! I can yet save you! Would you bring infamy on your sacred profession?' " Only when Dimmesdale has successfully resisted does Chillingworth openly reveal his purposes. With the physician the culminating irony is that in seeking to damn Dimmesdale he has himself fallen into damnation. As he says in a moment of terrible self-knowledge, " 'A mortal man, with once a human heart, has become a fiend for his especial torment!' " The effect is of an Aristotelian reversal, where a conscious and deep-laid purpose brings about totally unforeseen and opposite results. Chillingworth's relations with Dimmesdale have the persistent fascination of an almost absolute knowledge and power working their will with a helpless victim, a fascination which is heightened by the minister's awareness of an evil close beside him which he cannot place. "All this was accomplished with a subtlety so perfect that the minister, though he had constantly a dim perception of some evil influence watching over him, could never gain a knowledge of its actual nature." It is a classic situation wrought out to its fullest potentialities, in which the reader cannot help sharing the perverse pleasure of the villain.

From the victim's point of view the irony is still deeper, perhaps because we can participate still more fully in his response to it. Dimmesdale, a "remorseful hypocrite," is forced to live a perpetual lie in public. His own considerable talents for self-torture are supplemented by the situation as well as by the devoted efforts of Chillingworth. His knowledge is an agony. His conviction of sin is in exact relationship to the reverence in which his parishioners hold him. He grows pale and meager—it is the asceticism of a saint on earth; his effectiveness as a minister grows with his despair; he confesses the truth in his sermons, but transforms it "into the veriest falsehood" by the generality of his avowal and merely increases the adoration of his flock; every effort deepens his plight, since he will not—until the end—make the effort of complete self-revelation. His great election-day sermon prevails through anguish of heart; to his listeners divinely inspired, its power comes from its undertone of suffering, "the complaint of a human heart, sorrow-laden, perchance guilty, telling its secret, whether of guilt or sorrow, to the great heart of mankind. . . ." While Chillingworth at last reveals himself fully, Dimmesdale's secret is too great to be wholly laid bare. His utmost efforts are still partially misunderstood, and "highly respectable witnesses" interpret his death as a culminating act of holiness and humility.

Along with this steady irony of situation there is the omnipresent irony of the hidden meaning. The author and the reader know what the characters do not. Hawthorne consistently pretends that the coincidence of the action or the image with its significance is merely fortuitous, not planned, lest the effect be spoiled by overinsistence. In other words, he attempts to combine the sufficiently probable with the maximum of arrangement. Thus the waxing and waning of sunlight in the forest scene symbolize the emotions of Hester and Dimmesdale, but we accept this coincidence most easily if we can receive it as chance. Hawthorne's own almost amused awareness of his problem helps us to do so. Yet despite the element of play and the deliberate self-deception demanded, the total effect is one of intensity. Hawthorne is performing a difficult feat with sustained virtuosity in reconciling a constant stress between naturally divergent qualities.

The character of Pearl illuminates this point. Pearl is pure symbol, the living emblem of the sin, a human embodiment of the Scarlet Letter. Her mission is to keep Hester's adultery always before her eyes, to prevent her from attempting to escape its moral consequences. Pearl's childish questions are fiendishly apt; in speech and in action she never strays from the control of her symbolic function; her dress and her looks are related to the letter. When Hester casts the letter away in the forest,

Pearl forces her to reassume it by flying into an uncontrollable rage. Yet despite the undeviating arrangement of every circumstance which surrounds her, no single action of hers is ever incredible or inconsistent with the conceivable actions of any child under the same conditions. Given the central improbability of her undeviating purposiveness, she is as lifelike as the brilliantly drawn children of Richard Hughes's *The Innocent Voyage*.

These qualities of concentration, selectivity, and irony, which are responsible for the intensity of *The Scarlet Letter,* tend at their extreme toward excessive regularity and a sense of over-manipulation, although irony is also a counteragent against them. This tendency toward regularity is balanced by Hawthorne's use of ambiguity. The distancing of the story in the past has the effect of ambiguity. Hawthorne so employs the element of time as to warn us that he cannot guarantee the literal truth of his narrative and at the same time to suggest that the essential truth is the clearer; as facts shade off into the background, meaning is left in the foreground unshadowed and disencumbered. The years, he pretends, have winnowed his material, leaving only what is enduring. Tradition and superstition, while he disclaims belief in them, have a way of pointing to truth.

Thus the imagery of hell-fire which occurs throughout *The Scarlet Letter* is dramatically proper to the Puritan background and is attributed to the influence of superstitious legend. It works as relief from more serious concerns and still functions as a symbol of psychological and religious truth. In Chapter III, as Hester is returned from the scaffold to the prison, "It was whispered, by those who peered after her, that the scarlet letter threw a lurid gleam along the dark passage-way of the interior." The imagery of the letter may be summarized by quoting a later passage:

> The vulgar, who, in those dreary old times, were always contributing a grotesque horror to what interested their imaginations, had a story about the scarlet letter which we might readily work up into a terrific legend. They averred, that the symbol was not mere scarlet cloth, tinged in an earthly dye-pot, but was red-hot with infernal fire, and could be seen glowing all alight, whenever Hester Prynne walked abroad in the night-time. And we must needs say, it seared Hester's bosom so deeply, that perhaps there was more truth in the rumor than our modern incredulity may be inclined to admit.

The lightness of Hawthorne's tone lends relief and variety, while it nevertheless reveals the function of the superstition. "The vulgar," "dreary old times," "grotesque horror," "work up into a terrific legend''—his scorn is so heavily accented that it discounts itself and satirizes the ''modern incredulity'' of his affected attitude. The playful extravagance of ''red-hot with infernal fire'' has the same effect. And the apparent begrudging of the concession in the final sentence—''And we must needs say''—lends weight to a truth so reluctantly admitted.

Puritan demonology is in general used with the same effect. It has the pathos and simplicity of an old wives' tale and yet contains a deep subterranean power which reaches into daylight from the dark caverns of the mind. The Black Man of the unhallowed forest—a useful counterbalance to any too-optimistic picture of nature—and the witchwoman Mistress Hibbins are cases in point. The latter is a concrete example of the mingled elements of the superstitious legend. Matter-of-factly, she is a Puritan lady of high rank, whose ominous reputation is accounted for by bad temper combined with insanity. As a witch, she is a figure from a child's storybook, an object of delighted fear and mockery. Yet her fanciful extravagance covers a real malignity, and because of it she has an insight into the secret of the letter. With one stroke she lays bare the disease in Dimmesdale, as one who sees evil alone but sees it with unmatched acuteness: '' 'When the Black Man sees one of his own servants, signed and sealed, so shy of owning to the bond as is the Reverend Mr. Dimmesdale, he hath a way of ordering matters so that the mark shall be disclosed to the eyes of all the world.' ''

This use of the past merges into a deep-seated ambiguity of moral meaning. Moral complexity and freedom of speculation, like the lighter ambiguity of literal fact, temper the almost excessive unity and symmetry of *The Scarlet Letter* and avoid a directed verdict. In my opinion the judgment of Hawthorne upon his characters is entirely clear, although deliberately limited in its jurisdiction. But he permits the possibility of other interpretations to appear, so that the consistent clarity of his own emphasis is disguised. Let us take for example the consideration of the heroine in Chapter XIII, ''Another View of Hester.'' After seven years of disgrace, Hester has won the unwilling respect of her fellow-townsmen by her good works and respectability of conduct. From one point of view she is clearly their moral superior: she has met rigorous cruelty with kindness, arrogance with humility. Furthermore, living as she has in enforced isolation has greatly developed her mind. In her breadth of intellectual speculation she has freed herself from any dependence upon the laws of Puritan society. ''She cast away the fragments of a broken chain.'' She pays outward obedience to a system which has no further power upon her spirit. Under other conditions, Hawthorne suggests, she might at this juncture have become another Anne Hutchinson, the foundress of a religious sect, or a great early feminist. The author's conclusions about these possibilities, however, are specifically stated: "The scarlet letter had not done its office." Hester is wounded and led astray, not improved, by her situation. Hawthorne permits his reader, if he wishes, to take his character from his control, to say that Hester Prynne is a great woman unhappily born before her time, or that she is a good woman wronged by her fellow men. But Hawthorne is less confident.

In the multiple interpretations which constitute the moral ambiguities of *The Scarlet Letter* there is no clear distinction of true and false, but there *is* a difference between superficial and profound. In instances where interpretation of observed fact fuses with interpretation of moral meaning, conclusions are generally relative to those who make them. After Dimmesdale's climactic death scene:

> Most of the spectators testified to having seen, on the breast of the unhappy minister, a SCARLET LETTER—the very semblance of that worn by Hester Prynne—imprinted in the flesh. As regarded its origin, there were various explanations, all of which must necessarily have been conjectural. Some affirmed that the Reverend Mr. Dimmesdale, on the very day when Hester Prynne first wore her ignominious badge, had begun a course of penance,—which he afterwards, in so many futile methods, followed out,—by inflicting a hideous torture on himself. Others contended that the stigma had not been produced until a long time subsequent, when old Roger Chillingworth, being a potent necromancer, had caused it to appear, through the agency of magic and poisonous drugs. Others, again—and those best able to appreciate the minister's peculiar sensibility, and the wonderful operation of his spirit upon the body,—whispered their belief, that the awful symbol was the effect of the ever-active tooth of remorse, gnawing from the inmost heart outwardly, and at last manifesting Heaven's dreadful judgment by the visible presence of the letter.

Most singular is the fact that some spectators have seen no letter at all.

The presence of so many possibilities hints strongly that the whole truth is not to be found in any single choice, but Hawthorne's own preference is clearly indicated by "those best able to appreciate."

In a different case all interpretations are equally false, or at least equally erring. In Chapter XII, "The Minister's Vigil," a meteor flashes across the sky, which to the morbid eye of Dimmesdale takes the form of a gigantic *A*. This vision is attributed to the disordered mental state of the minister, though we cannot accept even this disclaimer with complete simplicity. This being the night of Governor Winthrop's death, one good old Puritan interprets the portent as *A* for Angel—an observation which has the effect of giving objective support to Dimmesdale's vision.

There is also the ambivalence of the Puritans. It is easy to pass them by too quickly. One's first impression is doubtless, as Hawthorne says elsewhere, of a set of "dismal wretches," but they are more than this. The Puritan code is arrogant, inflexible, overrighteous; and it is remarked of their magistrates and priests that "out of the whole human family, it would not have been easy to select the same number of wise and virtuous persons, who should be less capable of sitting in judgment on an erring woman's heart. . . ." Nevertheless, after finishing *The Scarlet Letter* one might well ask what merely human society would be better. With all its rigors, the ordeal of Hester upon the scaffold is invested with awe by the real seriousness and simplicity of the onlookers. Hawthorne compares the Puritan attitude, and certainly not unfavorably, to "the heartlessness of another social state, which would find only a theme for jest in an exhibition like the present." And it is counted as a virtue that the chief men of the town attend the spectacle without loss of dignity. Without question they take upon themselves more of the judgment of the soul than is fitting for men to assume, but this fault is palliated by their complete sincerity. They are "a people amongst whom religion and law were almost identical, and in whose character both were so thoroughly interfused, that the mildest and the severest acts of public discipline were alike made venerable and awful." By any ideal standard they are greatly lacking, but among erring humans they are, after all, creditable.

Furthermore, the vigor of Hawthorne's abuse of them is not to be taken at face value. They are grim, grisly, stern-browed and unkindly visaged; amid the gaiety of election day "for the space of a single holiday, they appeared scarcely more grave than most other communities at a period of general affliction." In this statement the tone of good-humored mockery is unmistakable. Hawthorne's attacks have something of the quality of a family joke; their roughness comes from thorough and even affectionate understanding. As his excellent critic and son-in-law G. P. Lathrop long ago pointed out, Hawthorne is talking of his own people and in hitting at them is quite conscious that he hits himself.

Finally, the pervasive influence of Hawthorne's style modifies the rigorous and purposeful direction of the action and the accompanying symmetrical ironies. The style is urbane, relaxed, and reposeful and is rarely without some touch of amiable and unaccented humor. This quality varies, of course, with the situation. Hester exposed on the scaffold and Dimmesdale wracked by Chillingworth are not fit subjects for humor. Yet Hawthorne always preserves a measure of distance, even at his most sympathetic. The effect of Hawthorne's prose comes partly from generality, in itself a factor in maintaining distance, as if the author at his most searching chose always to preserve a certain reticence, to keep to what is broadly representative and conceal the personal and particular. Even the most anguished emotion is clothed with decency and measure, and the most painful situations are softened by decorum.

Joel Porte

Redemption through Art

As Daniel Hoffman notes, the sprawling *House of the Seven Gables* manifestly lacks the taut economy of *The Scarlet Letter*. But Hoffman's allegation that Hawthorne's second major romance is without a "single controlling symbol like the letter" to unify its dispersed materials must certainly be disputed.[1] As with all of Hawthorne's books, the central symbol is signalled by the title, and its meaning is vitally connected with the implications of Hawthorne's art itself. *The House of the Seven Gables* can be read, with much less difficulty than is posed by the *The Scarlet Letter,* as a fable explaining the nature and function of romance.[2]

Fortunately, in *The House of the Seven Gables* the central meaning of the controlling symbol is made admirably clear by the author. On the first page we are told that there was something human about the house, and before long Hawthorne makes his meaning explicit:

> So much of mankind's varied experience had passed there—so much had been suffered, and something, too, enjoyed—that the very timbers were

[1] *Form and Fable in American Fiction,* p 187 The centrality of the house as well as the general unity of symbol and theme in the book are discussed by Maurice Beebe in "The Fall of the House of Pyncheon," *Nineteenth-Century Fiction,* XI (1956), 1–17.

[2] In "Who Killed Judge Pyncheon? The Role of the Imagination in *The House of the Seven Gables,*" *PMLA,* LXXI (1956), pp. 355–356, Alfred H. Marks argues that this is "the work in which [Hawthorne] is most serious in his devotion to the powers of beauty and the imagination. . . . the imagination is both subject matter and process: Hawthorne calls upon the reader to recognize the validity of imaginative truth by means of the imagination itself."

oozy, as with the moisture of a heart. It was itself like a great human heart, with a life of its own, and full of rich sombre reminiscences.

Later Hawthorne will confirm and expand the meaning of his symbol: as Phoebe prepares to leave temporarily the "heavy-hearted old mansion," she finds that every object in the place "responded to her consciousness, as if a moist human heart were in it." The house comes to stand for that "dungeon"—the individual heart—wherein the emotions of each of its inhabitants are imprisoned. And Hawthorne himself metaphorically poses the central problem of the book in a revealing passage near the end when, with Jaffrey Pyncheon lying dead at its core, the house is serenaded by an Italian organ-grinder: "The gloomy and desolate old house, deserted of life, and with awful Death sitting sternly in its solitude, was the emblem of many a human heart, which, nevertheless, is compelled to hear the trill and echo of the world's gaiety around it."

More important than this slightly fatuous meaning deceptively read out of the episode by the author himself is its true contextual significance. The Italian musician, who knows the "heart's language" and is elsewhere in the narrative elaborately presented as a type of the artist, is here trying with "pertinacity" to get the house to respond, to open up. "Will he succeed at last? Will that stubborn door be suddenly flung open?" The organ-grinder will of course not succeed in forcing the house to yield up the secret of its "inner heart," but his attempt—it will be successfully completed by another artist, Holgrave—symbolizes the major task of the romancer. Hawthorne is surely inviting us to recall his observation, in the preface to the tale, that it is the romancer's job to present the "truth of the human heart" and that this purpose is hopefully achieved in *The House of the Seven Gables* through an "attempt to connect a by-gone time with the very Present that is flitting away from us." The past of the house, the buried life, and the secrets of the heart are all caught up in one comprehensible metaphor that defines the function of the romancer.

The representative of Hawthorne's own art in the book is Holgrave, the daguerrèotypist—his very profession an emblem of that method of viewing reality at "one remove farther from the actual, and nearer to the imaginative," which for Hawthorne characterized romance—who presumably inherited from his Maule ancestors that power of imaginative insight into human nature, uneasily called "witchcraft" by the author, which is the dangerous gift of the artist. Like Hawthorne, who in Chapter 18 conjures up in the looking-glass ("which, you are aware, is always a kind of window or door-way into the spiritual world") a ghostly dumb show symbolic of the house's history which is a stylistic and thematic epitome of his book, the Maule posterity have a special relation to the magic glass:

> By what appears to have been a sort of mesmeric process—they could make its inner region all alive with the departed Pyncheons; not as they had shown themselves to the world, nor in their better and happier hours, but as doing over again some deed of sin, or in the crisis of life's bitterest sorrow.

Just such a "looking-glass" is Holgrave's own romance, the "legend" of Alice Pyncheon, which brings alive the sins and sorrows of the Pyncheons and almost mesmerizes poor Phoebe. (There is a "magnetic element" in Holgrave's nature that frightens Phoebe from the start, and the final elucidation of the house's mystery is obtained by Holgrave "from one of those mesmerical seers"—doubtless either himself or Hawthorne—"who, now-a-days, so strangely perplex the aspect of human affairs, and put everybody's natural vision to the blush, by the marvels which they see with their eyes shut.")

Like the romancer, the Maules control the symbolic world of dream and fantasy. ("The Pyncheons . . . , haughtily as they bore themselves in the noonday streets of their native town, were no better than bond-servants to these plebeian Maules, on entering the topsyturvy commonwealth of sleep.") The grandson of Matthew Maule "was fabled . . . to have a strange power of getting into people's dreams, and regulating matters there according to his own fancy, pretty much like the stage-manager of a theatre." This ability to conjure up and control the secrets of consciousness—in effect, insight into the human heart—is what licenses Holgrave to explore the darkest aspects of the house and empowers him finally to transform Phoebe into a mature, sexually aware woman. She may accuse him—after hearing him assert that it was not his impulse "to help or hinder; but to look on, to analyze, to explain matters to myself, and to comprehend the drama" of the house—of talking "as if this old house were a theatre" and of looking "at Hepzibah's and Clifford's misfortunes, and those of generations before them, as a tragedy . . . played exclusively for your amusement." But the romancer is necessarily committed to such a view, since his understanding of human nature is predicated on, and can only be expressed through, the refracting power of art. Hawthorne was, however, keenly aware of the danger—principally that of becoming a dilettante of symbolic gestures—lurking for the romance artist in his commitment to non-realistic modes of viewing and expressing human truth, and Phoebe's remark embodies his anxiety over such a danger. In another sense, Holgrave's tendency to aesthetic coldness might be considered the expression of an instinct of self-defense. The artist, reluctant to bear the dark knowledge that his art teaches, sometimes feels driven to treat that art as no more than an amusement. Indeed, for the sensitive Holgrave, the unattractive alternative to detachment seems to be a personal involvement in human suffering that leads to revulsion. "I dwell in it for a while," he says of the house, "that I may know the better how to hate it."

But there is also a possibility—the one which in fact opens up for Holgrave, as for Hester Prynne—that his painful knowledge of the human heart will carry him beyond smugness or misanthropy to the theory and practice of redemptive sympathy. And if Holgrave devotes himself to the art of romance only, as it would seem, to give it up at the end, his reluctant pursuit of his profession may be viewed as a reflection of Hawthorne's own dual attitude toward his art: his devotion to it and his desire to be released from its shadows. The intensity of this wish would enable him, by the time he came to write *The Marble Faun*, apparently to forget his previous productions and to insist that his own "dear native land" happily contained "no shadow, no antiquity, no mystery, no picturesque and gloomy wrong, nor anything but a common-place prosperity, in broad and simple daylight."

In the context of *The House of the Seven Gables* such an opinion is worthy only of the sunshiny hypocrisy of a Jaffrey Pyncheon, who, in his fear of romance truth and with his "hard, stern, relentless look," is directly opposed to the compassionate Holgrave, with his "deep, thoughtful, all-observant eyes," and to another artist figure, Clifford.[3] Like the other Pyncheon patriarchs, the Puritan Colonel and Gervayse, Jaffrey wants possession of the house so that he can exploit it to increase his worldly power: for him, the "secret" of the human heart is only another way to wealth. As for the true secret of his inner being, the "evil and unsightly thing" lurking at his core, he is devoted to keeping it "hidden from mankind,—forgotten by himself, or buried so deeply under a sculptured and ornamented pile of ostentatious deeds that his daily life could take no note of it." In a metaphoric tour de force which amounts to a defense of his art, Hawthorne implicitly invites us to compare with the romance sensibility (whose commitment to truth, however dark, expresses itself in the shaping and exploring of a *House*

---

[3]Rudolph Von Abele suggests "that Hawthorne is promulgating, in the Maule and Pyncheon family lines, images of the artist and the anti-artist in himself" (*The Death of the Artist*, p. 63). Alfred H. Marks contrasts Clifford's imaginative and spiritual nature with Jaffrey's coarse materiality.

of the Seven Gables) the "art" of Jaffrey Pyncheon—a glittering palace
of daylight fakery:

> Men of strong minds, great force of character, and a hard texture of the
> sensibilities, are very capable of falling into mistakes of this kind. They
> are ordinarily men to whom forms are of paramount importance. Their
> field of action lies among the external phenomena of life. They possess
> vast ability in grasping, and arranging, and appropriating to themselves,
> the big, heavy, solid unrealities, such as gold, landed estate, offices of
> trust and emolument, and public honors. With these materials, and with
> deeds of goodly aspect, done in the public eye, an individual of this class
> builds up, as it were, a tall and stately edifice, which, in the view of other
> people, and ultimately in his own view, is no other than the man's charac-
> ter, or the man himself. Behold, therefore, a palace! Its splendid halls and
> suites of spacious apartments are floored with a mosaic-work of costly
> marbles; its windows, the whole height of each room, admit the sunshine
> through the most transparent of plate-glass; its high cornices are gilded,
> and its ceilings gorgeously painted; and a lofty dome—through which,
> from the central pavement, you may gaze up to the sky, as with no
> obstructing medium between—surmounts the whole. With what fairer and
> nobler emblem could any man desire to shadow forth his character?

Despite its apparent splendor and solidity, however, this sunbathed
reality is a fraud. "In some low and obscure nook" lies "a corpse,
half-decayed, and still decaying, and diffusing its death-scent all
through the palace!" The inhabitant of the edifice is himself inured to
the stench, and his admirers are fooled by his cleverness and their own
willingness to be duped: "they smell only the rich odors which the
master sedulously scatters through the palace, and the incense which
they bring, and delight to burn before him!" But the romancer knows
the truth of the human heart: "Now and then, perchance, comes in a
seer, before whose sadly gifted eye the whole structure melts into thin
air, leaving only the hidden nook . . . and the decaying corpse
within."

Unlike the romancer, who builds his life on the sad but secure
knowledge of human guilt and pain reflected in the magic looking-glass
of his art, Jaffrey Pyncheon, "a hard, cold man . . . seldom or never
looking inward, and resolutely taking his idea of himself from what
purports to be his image, as reflected in the mirror of public opinion,
can scarcely arrive at true self-knowledge"—not even, the author suggests, at the final hour. As the governor-to-be lies inanimate in the
house, Hawthorne exhorts him repeatedly to return to life, saying—with
bitter irony—"ambition is a talisman more powerful than witchcraft."

But Jaffrey is, has been, and will always remain spiritually dead, as he is now physically so; his devotion to worldly ambition purchases him only eternal damnation. For it is the "witchcraft" of a Holgrave that is the true talisman. Romance, with all it implies, is shown in the meaning embedded at the heart of Hawthorne's tale to contain mankind's only real hope for re-entering Paradise.

This notion, along with Hawthorne's familiar metaphors for his art, is developed by Holgrave just after he has almost bewitched Phoebe by reading her his manuscript on Alice Pyncheon. As the moon begins "to shine out, broad and oval, in its middle pathway," everything, Hawthorne tells us, is "transfigured by a charm of romance," and Holgrave is inspired to propound his theory to that gentle Pyncheon descendant who, though "by nature as hostile to mystery, as the sunshine to a dark corner," is destined to redeem her race through her ultimate acceptance of the deepest mysteries of the heart:

> "After all, what a good world we live in! How good, and beautiful! How young it is, too, with nothing really rotten or age-worn in it! This old house, for example, which sometimes has positively oppressed my breath with its smell of decaying timber! And this garden, where the black mound always clings to my spade, as if I were a sexton delving in a graveyard! Could I keep the feeling that now possesses me, the garden would every day be virgin soil, with the earth's first freshness in the flavor of its beans and squashes; and the house!—it would be like a bower in Eden, blossoming with the earliest roses that God ever made. Moonlight, and the sentiment in man's heart, responsive to it, is the greatest of renovators and reformers."

Despite the schoolgirl gushiness of his exclamatory periods (he is, after all, a novice at literature), Holgrave's effusion has a vital relation to the book at large. His discovery that he really does not hate the house, when he sees it in the proper light, reflects Hawthorne's belief that romance has the power to transform the odor of decay and the sight of death into usable human truth. Tragedy, refracted through imagination, can redeem the fall of man into knowledge of good and evil by helping us to accept our "nastiness"—passion, cruelty, vice. Paradise will be regained only when art teaches us to accept our inner darkness as the quality that peculiarly defines the state of being human. It is as if Hawthorne were agreeing with the Calvinists that we are depraved, and yet insisting—with the artists and psychoanalysts—that we are not therefore culpable and worthy only of guilt and punishment.[4] The sadness

---

[4]"Moral and religious concerns," writes Hyatt H. Waggoner, "are almost always central in Hawthorne's work, but Hawthorne's interest in them is primarily subjective and psychological . . . existential" [*Nathaniel Hawthorne* (Minneapolis, 1962), p. 17].

attendant on our learning the secrets of sinful humanity (Paradise lost), as Holgrave goes on to explain to Phoebe, is the necessary prelude to adult rapture (Paradise regained).

> "I hardly think I understand you," said Phoebe.
>
> "No wonder," replied Holgrave, smiling; "for I have told you a secret which I hardly began to know, before I found myself giving it utterance. Remember it, however; and when the truth becomes clear to you, then think of this moonlight scene!"

Phoebe will shortly have a chance to test on her own pulses the validity of Holgrave's moonlight paradoxes when she is actually led by him into the heart of darkness—awareness of sex and death.

This new awareness can flower literally only over the dead body of Judge Jaffrey Pyncheon, the hypocritical representative of societal law, who has, as it were, banished the truth of the human heart from the House of the Seven Gables. Jaffrey's hostility toward the spirit of romance is emblematized in his attitude toward Clifford, "for whose character he had at once a contempt and a repugnance."[5] Clifford is clearly a type of the artist (in this case turned pitiful and self-indulgent because of the harshness of reality)—almost a caricature of Hawthorne himself. He has extremely delicate sensibilities, is in danger of falling into cold aestheticism, wants to live in the south of France or Italy, believes in mesmerism, is fond of blowing bubbles (Hawthorne calls them "brilliant fantasies," and in "The Custom-House" he referred to his own romance as a "soap-bubble"), and sees visions in Maule's well. Clifford, the living embodiment of human emotion (when Phoebe first heard his voice it seemed "less like articulate words than an un-shaped sound, such as would be the utterance of feeling and sympathy, rather than of the intellect"), is a "thunder-smitten Adam," driven from the once Edenic Garden of the house and imprisoned by the flaming sword of Judge Pyncheon's legal authority. Jaffrey not only hates Clifford but fears him, because Clifford is capable of discerning and exposing the brutal, aggressive nature hidden beneath Jaffrey's cloak of legality. For Jaffrey the truth of the human heart (his own) is ugly and must be suppressed; for Clifford it is painful, even terrible, but ultimately redemptive.

The sexual mentality of the two men is clearly contrasted by Hawthorne in their sharply different reactions to Phoebe's burgeoning womanhood. Watching her bud open into a blossom makes Clifford feel consciously lonely and melancholy, but he is able to accept his own

---

[5] "Clifford's artistic spirit is something the grasping spirit of the Pyncheons has placed in bondage," says Alfred H. Marks ("Who Killed Judge Pyncheon?" p. 367).

reaction to her deepening sexuality and turn his response to emotional use:

> His sentiment for Phoebe . . . was not less chaste than if she had been his daughter. . . . [But] he took unfailing note of every charm that appertained to her sex, and saw the ripeness of her lips, and the virginal development of her bosom. All her little, womanly ways, budding out of her like blossoms on a young fruit-tree, had their effect on him, and sometimes caused his very heart to tingle with the keenest thrills of pleasure.

Hawthorne obviously approves of the openness of Clifford's response and of his ability to convert "the fragrance of an earthly rosebud" into "visions of all the living and breathing beauty, amid which he should have had his home." Clifford—the artist as surrogate father —demonstrates the compatibility of love with authority when that authority is used, not to repress, but to make available and to direct the fullest human consciousness.

In the world of Jaffrey Pyncheon, however, sexuality is under a dark ban. Because it is seen as sinful, involving lechery, violation, and concomitant guilt, it must be repressed from public view—only to return as unabashed cruelty, first to others and finally to oneself (the gurgling, blood-in-the-throat death of the Pyncheon patriarchs), demonstrating that the price of self-deception is ultimate self-defeat. For Phoebe, the Judge is a kind of Electral ogre, the surrogate as ravishing father, whose inability to convert sexuality into tenderness serves to intimidate the developing woman. Meeting this "young rosebud of a girl" behind the counter of Hepzibah's cent-shop, Jaffrey offers to bestow "on his young relative a kiss of acknowledged kindred and natural affection," but for Phoebe "the man, the sex, somehow or other, was entirely too prominent," and she draws back from this "dark-browed, grisly bearded, white-neckclothed, and unctuously benevolent Judge." By "benevolence" Hawthorne clearly means to imply lust, since he tells us that the Judge's benevolence was "much like a serpent, which, as a preliminary to fascination, is said to fill the air with his peculiar odor." Thus surprised in the act of exhibiting his aggressive sexuality, Jaffrey's reaction is defensive—a hypocritical admonition that at once warns her off sex and cloaks his own exposed lust behind a mask of quasi-parental approval of her rejection:

> "I like that, Cousin Phoebe!" cried he, with an emphatic nod of approbation.—"I like it much, my little cousin! You are a good child, and know how to take care of yourself. A young girl—especially if she be a very pretty one—can never be too chary of her lips."

Denied an outlet for his sexuality, Jaffrey ends up retreating to repressive authority. Unlike the artist Clifford, whose easy and unthreatening acceptance of his own and Phoebe's sexuality inspires the girl to expose her womanhood and, as it were, makes secret emotions available for public use, the anti-artist Jaffrey serves to drive such emotions underground, whence they will reappear in a more sinister form.

Hawthorne makes it clear that behind the limitless evil-doing and malevolence of the old Puritan Pyncheon and his contemporary avatar lies a fund of hidden sexual cruelty.[6] But Phoebe, who belongs to "the trim, orderly, and limit-loving class," in order to avoid being "tumbled headlong into chaos" and "to keep the universe in its old place, was fain to smother, in some degree, her own intuitions as to Judge Pyncheon's character" and to discount Hepzibah's clear assertion of Jaffrey's infinite wickedness. Equipped only with her fragile "natural sunshine," Phoebe does not yet dare to exchange the apparent security of Jaffrey Pyncheon's law for the dark, and possibly dangerous, truths of the human heart. It will be the function of the "lawless mystic" Holgrave, girded with a "law of his own"—the romancer's imaginative insight—to lead Phoebe safely and lovingly into the inner sanctum of the house's secret. As Hawthorne suggests, Holgrave will play the Sybil to Phoebe's Aeneas, guiding her on the perilous journey to that Hades of the heart wherein reside all wisdom and power.

In *The House of the Seven Gables,* as in *The Marble Faun,* the one episode that can truly be called a love scene takes place in the presence of a corpse. Since a Poesque taste for necrophilia is totally alien to the spirit of Hawthorne's writing, we are forced to seek the meaning of this persistent motif otherwise than in the notion of a gratuitous dabbling with gothic horror. One thing at least is clear in *The House of the Seven Gables:* the death of the anti-romancer Jaffrey Pyncheon is the general signal for the release of all sorts of vital human energies. Art flourishes, love is consummated, and the protagonists are freed from the incubus of guilty subjection to a dark history; the bans on art, sex, and an understanding of the past are lifted all at once. Perhaps less clear at first glance is why Holgrave's leading Phoebe to knowledge of the corpse at the center of the house should be treated so momentously, and why that knowledge should be so intimately connected with their first real *pleasure* in each other. But the two questions can be answered together. Phoebe's introduction into an active awareness of death represents her introduction to knowledge of human evil—corruptibility—in others and at least potentially within herself, and the emotional and psychological

---

[6]Roy R. Male has commented on Jaffrey's "sexual brutality" (*Hawthorne's Tragic Vision,* p. 73).

depth obtained thereby will purchase her adult sexuality. It is this terrible job of deepening Phoebe's nature that is entrusted to the artist, Holgrave.

> [To him] it . . . seemed almost wicked to bring the awful secret . . . to her knowledge. It was like dragging a hideous shape into the cleanly and cheerful space before a household fire, where it would present all the uglier aspect, amid the decorousness of everything about it. Yet it could not be concealed from her; she must needs know it.

To mitigate the shock, Holgrave uses his art to present the corpse of Jaffrey to Phoebe at one remove, in a photographic image. But there is no mitigating the dark truth that our capacity for bearing tragedy and terror also measures our capacity for experiencing ecstasy—except as Holgrave had tried to prepare Phoebe in his moonlight theorizing. "In some cases," he had explained, "the two states come almost simultaneously, and mingle the sadness and the rapture in one mysterious emotion." Now, as he draws her into the secrets of love and death, he offers the "firm, but gentle and warm pressure" of his hand, "imparting a welcome which caused her heart to leap and thrill with an indefinable shiver of enjoyment."

"We must love one another or die," W. H. Auden has said notably with subdued irony, since we must die in any case. But the anxiety and terror engendered by the fact of death can be assuaged, and indeed compensated for, through sexual expression. Hawthorne accepts the full weight of the Miltonic truth that sex and death come into the world together, but he departs from Milton in proposing other than a purely religious solution to the problem. Our woe can be transformed into something like bliss, and the knowledge that kills can become the knowledge that cures, if only we can manage to cast off the nightmare of inherited guilt over our "corrupt" natures and achieve self-transcendence through sexual love. Symbolically joined in such a union of mutual acceptance and understanding, Phoebe and Holgrave are "conscious of nothing sad nor old. They transfigured the earth, and made it Eden again, and themselves the two first dwellers in it." Paradise is regained when the romance "truth of the human heart" is made available for Phoebe, and thus in some measure for society at large.

With the destruction of the "defunct nightmare" (Jaffrey), art itself is enabled to emerge from the shadows. "Alice's Posies" (the "one object" which Hawthorne hoped "would take root in the imaginative observer's memory"!)—palpable emblems of romance with their "crimson-spotted flowers," Italian origin, and affinity for the water from Maule's well—"were flaunting in rich beauty and full bloom, to-day, and seemed, as it were, a mystic expression that something within the house was consummated." Here again is the familiar association of successful romance art and sexual affirmation. But we should notice that the conclusion of Hawthorne's tale, besides celebrating the triumph of sexual love, also suggests that the Maule-Pyncheon marriage, with its simultaneous revelation and liquidation of the corpse of the past, will hopefully obviate much of the need for romance. The darkness has been dispersed, and compromise, in art as in life, is the order of the day. Now that his "lawlessness" has added a note of romance depth to Phoebe Pyncheon's law-abiding world view, Holgrave seems relieved to be able to renounce his witchcraft: "I have a presentiment, that, hereafter, it will be my lot to set out trees, to make fences—perhaps, even, in due time, to build a house for another generation—in a word, to conform myself to laws, and the peaceful practice of society.[7]

If Holgrave's promise to Phoebe is a covert expression of Hawthorne's own desire to be released from the burden of being a romancer, it may help to explain why he went on to write his next book. From a romance that ends by seemingly denying the future necessity for the form, Hawthorne moved on to a book that questions the aesthetic and moral premises of his own admittedly fantastic art [*The Blythedale Romance*].

[7]On Holgrave's "conversion" away from art see Rudolph Von Abele, *The Death of the Artist,* pp. 67–68.

Frederick Crews

Turning the Affair into a Ballad

> *"Le dessin est une espèce d'hypnotisme: on regarde tellement le modèle, qu'il vient s'asseoir sur le papier."* —Picasso

If *The Blithedale Romance* (1852), despite a good deal of recent explication, remains the least admired of Hawthorne's longer narratives, the reason is not far to seek. *The House of the Seven Gables* represented a drop in intensity from the sustained tragedy of *The Scarlet Letter,* but this next book seems to be divided between a drab chattiness and episodes of facile melodrama. Numerous passages are lifted, with scarcely any revision, from Hawthorne's Brook Farm notebooks. The narrator, Miles Coverdale, resembles his creator not only in superficial respects but in his fears about the unromantic, unpicturesque nature of modern life; his prose transcribes an incessant and labored effort to keep our interest. We are tempted to say that the book would have been better if it had been wholly devoted either to the autobiographical record of Hawthorne's disillusionment with Brook Farm utopianism or to the melodramatic and legendary events which are conjectured to form the prehistory of Coverdale's friends.

It would be wrong to sweep away these misgivings about *The Blithedale Romance* simply on the basis of a theory about its covert meaning; if the book has struck nearly all its readers as confused, then it is blameworthy. We are not surprised to learn that it was extensively rewritten and that Hawthorne, when he had finished, wondered whether to call it "Hollingsworth," "Zenobia," "Priscilla," "Miles Coverdale's Three Friends," "The Veiled Lady," "Blithedale," "The Arcadian Summer," or—his choice "in lack of a better"—"The Blithedale Romance."[1] Such indecision corresponds all too well to the indecisiveness of the story itself. *The Blithedale Romance* is a book in which Hawthorne's customary equivocation about social and moral ideas has been extended to include such apparently elementary matters as his moral estimate of his characters, his notion of their feelings about one another, and even his factual knowledge of their previous lives.

The view we have been taking of Hawthorne's career, however, leads us to expect that beneath the surface confusion of *The Blithedale Romance* there may be an inner coherence of self-debate. In the past we have found that Hawthorne's hesitations and implausibilities have always been the best indicators of obsessive thematic content; as the surface world becomes less intelligible its symbolic value becomes clearer. That this principle applies to the seeming chaos of the unfinished romances will be amply demonstrated. Yet *The Blithedale Romance* is just coherent enough to permit its critics to call it failed utopian satire or failed melodrama or failed autobiography. The necessity has rarely been perceived of putting the various imperfect parts within a single rationale that would explain Hawthorne's inability to make any one of them his focus of interest.

Our position is that *The Blithedale Romance* is, in an almost incredibly cryptic way, an intelligible product of the obsessed Hawthorne whose private themes have become so predictable. I believe we can justify the supposition that Hawthorne, finding his literal plot hopelessly distorted by irrational fantasy, turned the book into a self-critical comedy by attributing that distortion to his narrator. Like James in *The Sacred Fount,* perhaps, he partially rescued a doomed story by stressing the principle of self-delusion inherent in the narrator's—and ultimately in his own—prying concern with other lives. In neither case is the irony sufficiently unambiguous or sufficiently discernible to the reader; the most we can say is that it is consistently available to close scrutiny.

Certainly it is difficult to take the bewildering "romance" among Hollingsworth, Zenobia, and Priscilla as the heart of the book as it now stands. No narrator ever had worse luck than Coverdale in learning the most essential facts about the figures whose story we are supposed to

---

[1]See *The Memoirs of Julian Hawthorne,* ed. Edith Garrigues Hawthorne (New York, 1938), p. 34, and Hawthorne's *American Notebooks,* pp. 308f.

enjoy. Late in the plot he summarizes the points he has yet to settle, and indeed will never get straight at all: "Zenobia's whole character and history; the true nature of her mysterious connection with Westervelt; her later purposes towards Hollingsworth, and, reciprocally, his in reference to her; . . . the degree in which Zenobia had been cognizant of the plot against Priscilla, and what, at last, had been the real object of that scheme." Most of the important scenes he describes, furthermore, are observed from an inconvenient distance, or are not observed at all. Two of his chapters—Zenobia's legend of the Veiled Lady and the autobiography of her father, old Moodie—are imaginative reconstructions of someone else's words, and for the most crucial meeting of Hollingsworth, Zenobia, and Priscilla he arrives "half-an-hour too late."

These puzzling difficulties become significant when we realize that Hawthorne, and indeed Coverdale himself, have taken considerable pains to suggest that the story as we read it is not to be altogether trusted.[2] Repeatedly the narrator warns us that his descriptions may interest us not merely for their element of truth but "as exemplifying the kind of error into which my mode of observation was calculated to lead me." As soon as we put a friend under our microscope we "insulate him from many of his true relations, magnify his peculiarities, inevitably tear him into parts, and, of course, patch him very clumsily together again. What wonder, then, should we be frightened by the aspect of a monster, which, after all—though we can point to every feature of his deformity in the real personage—may be said to have been created mainly by ourselves!" This is, to be sure, a familiar Hawthornian paradox, but in *The Blithedale Romance* it appears to have been carried to a logical extreme. For Coverdale not only takes poetic liberties with the events he is narrating; he represents himself as having known how they would turn out before they occurred. His dreams and fantasies at Blithedale, if they had been recorded, "would have anticipated several of the chief incidents of this narrative, including a dim shadow of its catastrophe." It is impossible to say whether Coverdale has really had foreknowledge or has seriously altered the facts in recounting them; the only certain point is that we are meant to see some degree of correspondence between his tale and the secret inclination of his mind. From both ends of the plot—in apparent foreknowledge and in narrative distortion

[2]Some of the evidence for this and following statements may be found in my article, "A New Reading of *The Blithedale Romance*," *American Literature*, XXIX (May 1957), 147-70. My present view of the book, however, differs from the conclusions reached there.

—Coverdale shows us the condition of a man in the grip of some private symbolism.

Whatever the basis of Coverdale's obsession, the form it takes is literary. He imagines that his part has been "that of the Chorus in a classic play, which seems to be set aloof from the possibility of personal concernment, and bestows the whole measure of its hope or fear, its exultation or sorrow, on the fortunes of others, between whom and itself this sympathy is the only bond." Such aloofness is not to be confused with indifference; Coverdale is saying that he will allow his hope and fear to be expressed through his set of "characters," indeed, that is just what he calls them—"these three characters . . . on my private theatre." If in real life he is "but a secondary or tertiary personage" with his friends, and if "these three had absorbed [his] life into themselves," he at least has the artistic luxury of contemplating their worthiness for a "sufficiently tragic catastrophe." "After all was finished," he thinks with satisfaction, "I would come, as if to gather up the white ashes of those who had perished at the stake, and to tell the world—the wrong being now atoned for—how much had perished there which it had never yet known how to praise." Though "real life never arranges itself exactly like a romance," this is precisely what Coverdale has hoped to make of it—a Blithedale Romance. The abandonment of this hope, after it has been smashed by a real-life tragedy with no literary trimming, constitutes the true resolution of Hawthorne's plot.

To state the case in this manner is perhaps to underrate the obvious intellectual content of *The Blithedale Romance;* as most critics have chosen to emphasize, the book is Hawthorne's *apologia* for leaving Brook Farm and scorning its visionary ideals. I am certainly willing to believe that this was an important part of his intention when he began writing, but with Hawthorne self-justification invariably verges into self-criticism. What we in fact find in *The Blithedale Romance* is not so much a theoretical refutation of utopianism as an implied confession that the Hawthorne-Coverdale temperament is unsuited for real enterprises of any sort, whether spiritual or practical. One can abstract Coverdale's negative pronouncements about Blithedale into a body of social theory only by ignoring the intemperate sarcasm with which those pronouncements are delivered and the retractions that speedily follow them. Coverdale himself is aware, as Hawthorne's critics are often not, that all his contradictory opinions are dictated by his excessively self-conscious efforts to achieve a steady relation to his three "characters."

In order to understand Coverdale's complex situation it is not enough to see that he wants his three friends to act out a ready-made romance. Like other artist-heroes in Hawthorne's work he has a private failure of emotional capacity at the base of his need for aesthetic distance. He is the Hawthornian artist *par excellence:* a poetaster and a retiring bachelor whose emotions can be clearly expressed only within a womblike woodland "hermitage" where the voluptuous entanglement of vines and trees is conducive to spying at secret *rendezvous* and daydreaming about artistic and erotic successes that will never be realized. "Had it ever been my fortune to spend a honey-moon," he explains, "I should have thought seriously of inviting my bride up thither"—namely, into "a hollow chamber, of rare seclusion . . . formed by the decay of some of the pine-branches, which the vine had lovingly strangled with its embrace." And yet the speaker of these lines—eloquent as they are in declaring his oneness with the sexual eccentrics who dominate Hawthorne's tales—tells us, when his "romance" has collapsed, that he was in love with Priscilla all along. Whether or not we are prepared to take the statement at face value, its insertion at the last possible moment is characteristic of the erotic furtiveness which pervades the narrative.

Thus we cannot rest content with the view of Coverdale adopted by Hollingsworth, who accuses him of feigning interest in utopianism only because "it has given you a theme for poetry," nor with the similar charge brought by Zenobia: "You are turning this whole affair into a ballad." These are half-truths which exaggerate the definiteness of Coverdale's intention and the steadiness of his aesthetic detachment. The cumulative evidence of Coverdale's own statements suggests that he cannot decide whether to win his companions' affection or to pry coldly into "the secret which was hidden even from themselves." Generally speaking, what happens in the plot is that Coverdale, harboring this uncertainty of purpose, half-intentionally alienates all three of his potential intimates and is thus driven increasingly into the role of literary snoop. Hollingsworth, Zenobia, and Priscilla become, no longer human companions, but "goblins of flesh and blood" from whom he would like to escape—but from whom he simultaneously wants to extort "some nature, some passion, no matter whether right or wrong, provided it were real." And correspondingly, his fantasies become at once more destructive and more literary as he is continually rebuffed. Well before the real tragedy of the book occurs, Coverdale

> began to long for a catastrophe. If the noble temper of Hollingsworth's soul were doomed to be utterly corrupted by [his] purpose . . .; if the rich and generous qualities of Zenobia's womanhood might not save her; if

Priscilla must perish by her tenderness and faith . . .; then be it so! Let it all come! As for me, I would look on, as it seemed my part to do, understandingly. . . . The curtain fallen, I would pass onward with my poor individual life, which was now attenuated of much of its proper substance. . . .

This vengeful daydream recalls the consolations of other embittered artists in Hawthorne's fiction. Having survived his indifferent friends and emptied himself of concern for them (even at the price of losing all further meaning in his life), Coverdale will have the luxury of contemplating their doom "reverently and sadly."

Though it is impossible to draw a point-by-point comparison between the actual course of events and Coverdale's fantasies, we can observe that the real calamity of the plot makes Coverdale profoundly ashamed of those fantasies. This may suggest that something more is involved than mere disappointment of the wish to win Priscilla. Like some previous heroes Coverdale is made to feel guilty, or at any rate chastened, about a death he has not caused but has hazily "foreseen" in fantasy. It seems plausible to assume that one component of his feelings toward Zenobia—namely, the anxiety that has made the pale Priscilla a safer object of desire—has found the thought of her removal advantageous. Or we could surmise, with equal likelihood, that it is Hollingsworth, his rival for the affection of both women, against whom Coverdale's aggressive prophecies have been intended. In either case Coverdale has indeed anticipated "a dim shadow of the catastrophe" of his Blithedale Romance, and is jolted by the shocking explicitness of that catastrophe when it occurs.

Coverdale himself has no clear idea of why Hollingsworth, Zenobia, and Priscilla together are more meaningful to him than his relation to any one of them individually. And yet our awareness of the fantasies chronically harbored by Hawthorne's escapists may make us attentive to some revealing clues. Hawthorne and Coverdale have virtually begged us to see the story of Coverdale's friends—not just his attitude toward it, but the bare facts of the story itself—as indicative of the inmost tendency of his mind. That story, we must emphasize, is intricately involved in family matters of a vaguely guilty nature. The sexual rivals, Zenobia and Priscilla, turn out to be half-sisters. Their remorseful benefactor, old Moodie, is revealed to be their common father, who has neglected the child he loved best in order to live vicariously in the other child's splendor. The devilish mesmerist Westervelt, the touchstone of evil in *The Blithedale Romance,* is said to be Zenobia's former husband. He is thus related, however remotely, to the

Priscilla who is perhaps turned over to his mesmeric power through the contrivance of Zenobia herself—a fine example of Hawthornian family co-operation. Priscilla's rescue in turn is effected by the noble Hollingsworth, who, though he has hitherto loved her like "an elder brother," promptly marries her.[3]

These facts alone cannot be called proof that the furtiveness and ambivalence of Coverdale's attitudes may be related to a preoccupation with incest. Yet that speculation begins to seem more respectable as we examine the specific feelings his three friends arouse in him. The brash and bosomy feminist Zenobia, Coverdale's first and most deeply engaging figure of challenge, incites anxiety and defensive sarcasm by flaunting her sexuality before him. Her provocative language forces him to picture "that fine, perfectly developed figure, in Eve's earliest garment"—a vision not entirely welcome to a nature like Coverdale's. The significant fact, however, is that he can scarcely accept the blatantly obvious fact of her sexual experience, but must dwell on the question with prurient concern: "Pertinaciously the thought—'Zenobia is a wife! Zenobia has lived, and loved! There is no folded petal, no latent dewdrop, in this perfectly developed rose'—irresistibly that thought drove out all other conclusions, as often as my mind reverted to the subject." This dainty pornography is continually rejected as "a masculine grossness—a sin of wicked interpretation, of which man is often guilty towards the other sex." The absurdity of such scrupulous fancies is diminished if we bear in mind that Zenobia is, for Coverdale's mind, less an individual person than "womanliness incarnated," and that his view of this womanliness is rather that of a scandalized son than a sophisticated bachelor. Like his younger predecessors Goodman Brown and Robin Molineux, Coverdale has not yet forgiven womankind for its deviation from the maternal ideal.

If Zenobia is to this extent eligible for sentiments that should properly attach themselves to a mother, Hollingsworth is more easily recognized as a version of the Hawthornian father. Though Coverdale is forced to respect him and yearn for his affection, the physically impos-

---

[3] Even the nature of Priscilla's affection for Zenobia seems a bit perverse if we follow the implications of Hawthorne's imagery: "Priscilla's love grew, and twined itself perseveringly around this unseen sister; as a grape-vine might strive to clamber out of a gloomy hollow among the rocks, and embrace a young tree, standing in the sunny warmth above." The echo of Coverdale's "perfectly inextricable knot of polygamy" in his tree-vine hermitage casts a metaphorical suspicion of fixated emotion even on the vapid Priscilla—or perhaps merely on Coverdale's interest in her. An article by Allan and Barbara Lefcowitz [*Nineteenth-Century Fiction*, 21 (1966), 263–75] explores the remarkable sexual innuendoes surrounding Priscilla's role as a mesmeric clairvoyant and a maker of tiny purses.

ing, fiercely stern and fanatical Hollingsworth drains life from everyone who must live under his authority, and more particularly usurps all the feminine sympathy that Coverdale himself seeks. In retrospect it seems inevitable that he must eventually appear to Coverdale in the stereotyped role of the Hawthornian father, as "the grim portrait of a Puritan magistrate, holding inquest of life and death in a case of witch-craft." The transformation has been anticipated since Coverdale's first confession that he feels a need to exaggerate Hollingsworth's awesome-ness: "In my recollection of his dark and impressive countenance, the features grew more prominent than the reality, duskier in their depth and shadow, and more lurid in their light; the frown, that had merely flitted across his brow, seemed to have contorted it with an adamantine wrinkle." Here we are observing Coverdale in the process of creating a bogey-father, a devil; and significantly, the true "devil" of *The Blithedale Romance,* Westervelt, is held responsible for having de-stroyed Zenobia's much-lamented innocence.

As for Priscilla, she is literally a sister, she looks like a sister, she is loved like a sister by Hollingsworth, and she inspires protective brotherly feelings—mixed with an erotic desire which is confessed later—on Coverdale's part. The shunting of that desire from Zenobia to her is nothing more than what is demanded by Freudian logic and Hawthornian precedent. Her integral role in Coverdale's fantasy-family is indicated by his most revealing dream: "Hollingsworth and Zenobia, standing on either side of my bed, had bent across it to exchange a kiss of passion. Priscilla, beholding this—for she seemed to be peeping in at the chamber-window—had melted gradually away, and left only the sadness of her expression in my heart." The reader who doubts that Coverdale has unconsciously cast himself as a son must wonder why this dream depicts Hollingsworth and Zenobia in the unorthodox erotic pose of bending across Coverdale's bed. And all readers must surely note the moral ambiguity of the wish expressed in the dream. Priscilla is meant to be disillusioned by the sexual passion which she has discov-ered in her elders, yet Coverdale's own intentions toward her, as we later discern, are those of a lover. As in the unfinished romances, where real brothers and sisters are forever about to become lovers or spouses, the image of Priscilla-detached-from-Hollingsworth melts away before its purpose in Coverdale's mental scenario becomes too plain.

In all this, it may be objected, there is no compelling evidence that Coverdale's hesitant designs on Priscilla, and more distantly on Zenobia, are incestuous in quality. I agree. What we find is, on one side, an extraordinary deviousness in his approach to both women, and on the other a configuration of attitudes which, if discovered in a real neurotic, would point to incestuous fixation. A man of mature years who dwells with awe and titillation on the possibility that a mature woman may not be virginal, who must suppose that her experience has been at the hands of a fiendish seducer, who hopes for the love of a sexless girl but can do nothing to win her, and who turns his sexual rival into an imaginary paternal tyrant—such a man must justly be called a casualty of Oedipal strife. The real difficulty in applying this reasoning to Coverdale is that the literal reality surrounding him conforms so well to his apparent fixation. We must assume, as so often in the past, that the obsession of *The Blithedale Romance* is jointly owned by the hero and the author. And this assumption is necessary anyway if we are to accept without astonishment the intricacy and secrecy of self-debate in this book. If Hawthorne has blurred all his portraits except Coverdale's, backed away from the simplest explanations of fact, exploited literal scenes for a cabalistic meaning that is lost upon the reader, and included episodes that make virtually no sense apart from such meaning, then we must infer that Hawthorne as well as Coverdale is at the mercy of unconscious logic.

In that logic, *spiritual aspiration, reform of humanity,* and *romantic art* are interchangeable terms; each represents flight from mature sexual challenge. The touchstone of that challenge, and the implicit reproach to all escapism in *The Blithedale Romance,* is Zenobia, whose womanly nature is equally spurned in the poetic fancies of Coverdale and the zealous perfectionism of Hollingsworth. "The presence of Zenobia," Coverdale admits, "caused our heroic enterprise to show like an illusion, a masquerade, a pastoral, a counterfeit Arcadia, in which grown-up men and women were making a play-day of the years that were given us to live in." In our view it is far from insignificant that the whole Blithedale colony should be accused of regression to childhood. Unconsciously, no doubt, Coverdale is well equipped to grasp the primitive sameness of motive among all attempts to beautify human nature. Nor is it surprising that the event which signals an end to both Coverdale's and Blithedale's picturesque fancies is the death of Zenobia; the *raison d'être* for all such fancies is avoidance of the object of anxiety that has been too violently removed.

If acceptance of Zenobia is the measure of normality in *The Blithedale Romance,* the opposite psychological extreme is embodied in Westervelt. Cynic, fraud, and unscrupulous possessor of a young girl's will, he partakes of Ethan Brand, of Rappaccini, of Goodman Brown's devil. "A part of my own nature," says Coverdale frankly, "showed itself responsive to him." Coverdale's latent sense of mankind's corruption—a sense whose sexual basis we have tried to suggest—is fully developed in Westervelt. Both men are show-masters of a sort, and both use the rhetoric of ideality to conceal their aversion to humanity. Both in fact are trying to present the same "Veiled Lady," Priscilla, in a magical and romantic light which they know to be fakery. Both, too, are snoopers; the real difference is that Westervelt knows the facts that Coverdale hankers to learn. If Coverdale is appalled by Westervelt's mockery of him, he nevertheless finds himself drawn ever closer to the idea of getting Westervelt's precious information. If Westervelt is a devil, it is Miles Coverdale who, surrounded by a band of masqueraders who parody his dissociation from reality, is accused of being "always ready to dance to the devil's tune." When Coverdale actually attends one of Westervelt's mesmeric sessions and sees the anti-poet Hollingsworth rush onto the stage to rescue Priscilla from her part in a vulgar and fraudulent art form, the defeat applies as much to Coverdale as to Westervelt. At the end of the book both men are unemployed mesmerists, deprived, by a real marriage, of their "subjects" for the showmanship of repression.

The structure of *The Blithedale Romance* may be appreciated if we picture two opposite lines of development. Coverdale, beginning with hopes of establishing human intimacy with his Blithedale friends, moves more or less steadily in the direction of Westervelt's alienation, cynicism, and artistic quackery. His real "characters," meanwhile, begin in pastoral attitudes and utopian fancies but become progressively more eligible for the tragic denouement which in fact occurs. By the time Coverdale, nearly maddened by his failure as a man and by the failure of reality to be adequately romantic, stumbles upon Hollingsworth, Zenobia, and Priscilla in their real scene of parting, he is so abashed by "the intentness of their feelings" that he feels "no right to be or breathe there."[4] Just when his literary material has become "all that an artist could desire," Coverdale repents of art. When Hollings-

---

[4]Coverdale is "left to my own conjectures" about the terms of the falling-out between Hollingsworth and Zenobia, and the diligent reader cannot get much farther than Coverdale does in divining the omitted truth. It seems that Hollingsworth has accused Zenobia of some misdeed, perhaps the betrayal of her own sister into Westervelt's hands. In the scene we witness, however, Zenobia makes the same accusation against Hollingsworth, who now professes love for Priscilla. We can, however, surmise why Hollingsworth has switched his attentions from Zenobia to Priscilla. Their sisterhood has been revealed, and at the same time Zenobia has learned that she is not to inherit the fortune she supposed —meaning, I gather, that Moodie has avenged Priscilla's ill-treatment by making her his heiress. Thus the logical zealot Hollingsworth has simply continued his policy of courting the lady who can pay for his philanthropic project. It seems to me that Coverdale has some notion of this, for he spends a whole paragraph reflecting on Zenobia's willful incapacity to see the worst side of Hollingsworth's motives.

worth departs with Priscilla, Coverdale is free at last to give Zenobia some genuine sympathy; for the two of them have been simultaneously deprived of a love-object and a romantic dream. It is too late for Coverdale to prevent her suicide, but he can at least answer with a clear conscience when she bursts out, "Ah, I perceive what you are about! You are turning this whole affair into a ballad. Pray let me hear as many stanzas as you happen to have ready!" "Oh, hush, Zenobia!" he answers, in his nearest approach to human warmth; "Heaven knows what an ache is in my soul!"

The chapter that follows Zenobia's somewhat histrionic farewell to Coverdale is generally acknowledged as the strongest portion of *The Blithedale Romance*. Never again, after this scene of three men grimly probing for Zenobia's corpse in a river pool at midnight, was Hawthorne to write so vividly. Here for once Hawthorne-Coverdale has no need of irony or apology for serving up fantasy as if it were truth; the spectacle is so stark that after twelve years Coverdale can "reproduce it as freshly as if it were still before my eyes." The counterpointing of Silas Foster's Yankee banalities against the intrinsic horror of the scene is Shakespearian in effect. All affectation has been dismissed —including the affectation of tragedy. Zenobia, Coverdale finds himself reflecting despite himself, must have seen many a sentimental picture of wronged village maidens who had drowned themselves "in lithe and graceful attitudes." Had she been able to anticipate the hideous rigidity of her corpse, "she would no more have committed the dreadful act, than have exhibited herself to a public assembly in a badly-fitting garment." This is the end of romance, not only for Zenobia but for Coverdale as well. The frank brutality of the chapter amounts to a devastating commentary on all "spiritual" attitudinizing—Coverdale's, Blithedale's, and, we might add, the future attudinizing of *The Marble Faun*.

Certainly the power of this chapter has much to do with Hawthorne's memory of a similar episode in his own life. To say this, however, is not to explain why the scene consummates the whole progress of *The Blithedale Romance*. The image of Zenobia in death has been anticipated—literally anticipated by the "nameless presentiment" which led Coverdale to the river bank, and anticipated in imagery by all the symbolic rigmarole about the veiling of truth. When blunt Silas Foster states the likelihood that Zenobia has drowned, it is "as if he were removing the napkin from the face of a corpse." Surely we are meant to recall, at this moment of supreme reality, "the face of a corpse" which the hero of Zenobia's own tale of a Veiled Lady imagined beneath the veil. That hero risked losing a beautiful woman's love rather than kiss the "virgin lips" beneath the veil; he imagined the unseen visage to be, not only a corpse, but "the grinning cavity of a monster's mouth" or "a monstrous visage, with snaky locks, like Medusa's, and one great red eye in the centre of the forehead."[5] Zenobia's body has been the source of all curiosity, all squeamishness, and all regressive flight up to this point. In probing with a hooked pole into the "broad, black, inscrutable depth" of the pool, Hollingsworth makes "precisely such thrusts . . . as if he were stabbing at a deadly enemy"—the knife-thrusts of Aylmer's dream. Zenobia at the bottom of the black pool is yet another petrified Digby in his overgrown cave. If "reality" has the last word in *The Blithedale Romance,* it is not the humdrum reality that Coverdale has found both irritating and secretly comforting, but the conjunction of a factual event with the worst sadistic fantasy.

So, too, Coverdale's emotions when he studies the corpse remain consistent with his Oedipal preoccupation. Neither he nor Zenobia has hitherto shown a sincere interest in religion,[6] yet her last inflexible pose makes Coverdale wonder about the fate of her soul:

> One hope I had; and that, too, was mingled half with fear. She knelt, as if in prayer. With the last, choking consciousness, her soul, bubbling out through her lips, it may be, had given itself up to the Father, reconciled and penitent. But her arms! They were bent before her, as if she struggled against Providence in never-ending hostility. Her hands! They were clenched in immitigable defiance. Away with the hideous thought! The flitting moment, after Zenobia sank into the dark pool—when her breath was gone, and her soul at her lips—was as long, in its capacity of God's infinite forgiveness, as the lifetime of the world.

Zenobia's imagined defiance of the "Father" makes little sense in terms of anything we have been told about her religion, but it makes perfect sense if we may assume that the thought of reconciliation to a heavenly Father is bound up with feelings toward an earthly father or father-surrogate. This is the case, we recall, in "The Gentle Boy,"

---

[5]For psychoanalytic interpretations of the Medusa figure without Hawthorne's untraditional but appropriate extra detail, see Freud, *Collected Papers,* V. 105f., and Sándor Ferenczi, *Further Contributions to the Theory and Technique of Psycho-Analysis* (London, 1960), p. 360.

[6]See, however, the following early reflection of Coverdale's, which is pertinent both to the present scene and to *The Marble Faun:* "I have always envied the Catholics their faith in that sweet, sacred Virgin Mother, who stands between them and the Deity, intercepting somewhat of His awful splendor, but permitting His love to stream upon the worshipper, more intelligibly to human comprehension, through the medium of a woman's tenderness."

"Young Goodman Brown," "Rappaccini's Daughter," and "Roger Malvin's Burial." Hollingsworth, the obvious target of Zenobia's spite in committing suicide, is to blame for her death, yet Coverdale—as befits the Hawthornian protagonist who has never emerged from emotional childhood—concerns himself only with whether the father has now been sufficiently appeased. His "faith," like Hawthorne's at his mother's deathbed, is inspired by a hope that the heavenly Father may not be as cruel as he patently appears.[7] Providence has proved sadistic, the impulse to defiance persists, and *therefore* he must fearfully hope that all will be well. Hollingsworth in the previous chapter has been sent a final rebellious message by Zenobia—"Tell him he has murdered me! Tell him that I'll haunt him!"—and in the following chapter Coverdale will goad him in his misery "with a bitter and revengeful emotion." No wonder, then, that Coverdale finds it so hard (and so urgently necessary) to persuade himself that Zenobia has made her peace with the Father above.

The very sincerity of Coverdale's anguish may explain why his scene of truly effective drama is presented as something beyond the scope of his art. Zenobia's body is in a sense a perfectly mimetic artifact: "She was the marble image of a death-agony." But neither Coverdale nor Hawthorne can sustain, or indeed tolerate, an art of sordid truthfulness; as Coverdale has earlier complained about a painting of a drunken man on a bench, "The death-in-life was too well portrayed." Hawthornian art is necessarily an art of ideality, of flight from unacceptable truth. It becomes psychologically penetrating and aesthetically "right" only to the degree that the repressed is allowed to return *within the bounds of characterization,* as in the monomaniacs of the better tales. When, in *The Marble Faun,* characterization stays on the level of sentimental convention while the imagery shrieks of incest, Hawthorne's art is effectively finished. What we see in Zenobia's death is the unmanageable hideousness that Hawthorne will henceforth try to keep wholly out of view.

With this knowledge in mind we may place some importance on an

---

[7] "Oh what a mockery," Hawthorne confided to his notebook, "if what I saw were all . . . But God would not have made the close so dark and wretched, if there were nothing beyond; for then it would have been a fiend that created us, and measured out our existence, and not God. It would be something beyond wrong—it would be insult—to be thrust out of life into annihilation in this miserable way. So, out of the very bitterness of death, I gather the sweet assurance of a better state of being" *(American Notebooks,* p. 210). Hawthorne's celebrated faith was never more sincerely cherished, I imagine, than here; yet the passage says in effect that he must believe in order to stifle his outrage at what he has witnessed. He will be a better Christian by his terror of the atheistic thoughts he cannot silence.

otherwise inconspicuous fact: Coverdale at the end follows his immediate predecessor Holgrave in renouncing art and gaining a measure of mental peace. The two successive palinodes prepare us for the Hawthorne who was to complete only one intricately self-defeating romance in the twelve years that were left to him, and for the Hawthorne who said of *Mosses from an Old Manse* in 1854, "Upon my honor, I am not quite sure that I entirely comprehend my own meaning in some of these blasted allegories. . . . I am a good deal changed since those times; and to tell you the truth, my past self is not very much to my taste, as I see myself in this book."[8] *The Blithedale Romance* is Hawthorne's cunning farewell to that "past self" which was responsible for all his greatest fiction. Half understanding and wholly disapproving of the nature of Coverdale's artistic purposes, Hawthorne was able to rise for the last time to the level of sustained self-criticism. The aftermath will be sheer evasion.

[8]Letter to Fields, quoted by Stewart, *American Notebooks,* p. 332n.

John Caldwell Stubbs

The Marble Faun: *Hawthorne's Romance of the Adamic Myth*

The Marble Faun is a curiously modern book. Generally, critics have not recognized that fact and have tended to ask the wrong questions about the work and to express dissatisfaction with it for the wrong reasons. My contention is that *The Marble Faun* is Hawthorne's final experiment with methods of creating the artistic distance of romance and using artifice to probe self-consciously for meaning. In this work he interests himself singlemindedly with fabricating the substance and texture of archetypal myth. Surely we can all agree that the work is flawed. It is too prolix. Like the American tourist with his slide collection, Hawthorne has brought back too many recollections of Italy. But our basis for discussing its flaws ought to reside in our seeing it as an experiment with the presentation of myth. For Hawthorne *The Scarlet Letter* was a culminating effort with the form of the historical romance. In *The House of the Seven Gables* and *The Blithedale Romance* he turned to comedy and to irony as modes to work with. Now myth.

Hawthorne's kind of experimentation in *The Marble Faun* ought to be obvious to us, because it is exactly the kind of experimentation with artifice going on among modern, anti-realist writers. Consider, for example, the remarks of John Hawkes, author of *The Lime Twig* and *The Second Skin:*

> My novels are not highly plotted, but certainly they are elaborately structured. I began to write fiction on the assumption that the true enemies of

From The Pursuit of Form: A Study of Hawthorne and the Romance *by John Caldwell Stubbs. Copyright © 1970 by the Board of Trustees of the University of Illinois. Revised by the author for publication here and reprinted by his permission and that of the University of Illinois Press.*

the novel were plot, character, setting, and theme, and having once abandoned these familiar ways of thinking about fiction, *totality of vision* or
structure was really all that remained. And structure—*verbal and
psychological coherence*—is still my largest concern as a writer. Related
or corresponding event, recurring image and recurring action, these constitute the essential substance or meaningful density of my writing [italics
mine].[1]

Hawkes claims accurately of his own work that he has stripped away
concern with plot and character. So has Hawthorne. That characters of
both are not "round" is irrelevant to the aims of both writers. And
Hawthorne's conclusion added to the second edition of *The Marble
Faun* makes clear that he, like the modern writer, has little interest in
working out the details of plot. Hawthorne differs from Hawkes in his
emphasis on setting and theme. Assuredly these are most important
elements to Hawthorne. But they are important mainly as they contribute to what Hawkes calls "totality of vision" or the structure of
"verbal and psychological coherence." Hawthorne's aim is to create a
world of myth, related to our world but universal and separate. He
draws heavily on "related or corresponding event, recurring image and
recurring action" to make up the texture of that world. The use of
setting, almost always symbolic as well as descriptive of the Italian
scene, and the use of theme, in itself a kind of "recurring action" in
The Marble Faun, contribute mightily to that world he makes. So it is
the texture and meaning of the *total vision,* the mythic construct, we
must examine.

The romance is an endless series of repetitions and balances. Virtually every action and every symbolic object are reflected over and
over as if caught in two facing mirrors. Each comes to us with a "sense
of ponderous remembrances" demonstrably attached, or else it stands
against a contrasting action or object. In other words, the progress of the
book stems from association and contrast. These are properties we most
often think of as operating in the flow of the subjective mind, particularly in a dream. Of course in modified form they are staples of all
fiction. However, the point is that in *The Marble Faun* they do not
appear in modified form; rather, they are the guiding principles of the
work's coherence. Beside them character and plot count for very little.
We should not be surprised to find Hawthorne dealing with a dreamlike
texture. In 1842, he expressed the desire to write a work that was totally
dreamlike: "To write a dream, which shall resemble the real course of a

[1]Hawkes, "John Hawkes: An Interview," *Wisconsin Studies in Contemporary Literature,* VI (Summer, 1965), 149.

dream, with all its inconsistency, its strange transformations, which are all taken as a matter of course, its eccentricities and aimlessness—with nevertheless a leading idea running through the whole. Up to this old age of the world, no such thing ever has been written." This statement, written eighteen years before the publication of *The Marble Faun,* is perhaps the best gloss on its technique that Hawthorne could have given us. In this work we are aware of the artist's mind, or a general disembodied mind behind the work, moving dreamlike toward the total vision of a myth.

The principles Hawthorne used to create the dreamlike texture, the principles of balance and repetition, are established at the outset through art objects.[2] The romance opens in the sculpture gallery in the Capitol at Rome with the four major characters engaged in a dispute over whether Donatello is a living replica of the Marble Faun attributed to Praxiteles. Through the comparison, Hawthorne at once puts Donatello into a pattern of symbols recurring through time. Donatello recalls an image from the Arcadian Age before the founding of Rome, and he recalls an image of a conception that occurred to the sculptor of the Greek-Roman Age in which the statue was made. Along with this sense of an image repeated through history comes the sense of counterpoint, established during the first paragraph, in the statue of the Human Soul "with its choice of Innocence or Evil close at hand, in the pretty figure of a child, clasping a dove to her bosom, but assaulted by a snake." As the book continues, each of the major characters has contrasting art objects associated with him.

Kenyon's masterpiece is his statue of Cleopatra. It is a masterpiece because in it Kenyon portrays rich and complex human emotions. Cleopatra is caught in repose—"between two pulse-throbs." Yet, as Hawthorne puts it, "such was the creature's latent energy and fierceness, she might spring upon you like a tigress, and stop the very breath that you were now drawing, midway in your throat."[3] The statue represents Kenyon's understanding, perhaps intuitive only, of human passion. A contrasting side of Kenyon's nature, however, is shown in the small, delicately sculptured marble hand he has done. It is modeled on Hilda's hand; and Kenyon keeps it, reverently, in an ivory coffer. For

[2]Two recent critics have argued that the art objects do much more than set the scene: Paul Brodtkorb, Jr., "Art Allegory in *The Marble Faun*," *PMLA*, LXXVII (June, 1962), 254–267; and Frederick W. Turner, III, "Hawthorne and the Myth of Paradise," *Serif*, III (September, 1966), 9–12. Brodtkorb finds an art allegory in the work, with Hilda representing the spirit of art or art's ideality and timelessness. Turner argues just the opposite. He finds that art as an embodiment of knowledge is an agent of Donatello's fall.

[3]*The Marble Faun: or, The Romance of Monte Beni,* Centenary Edition (Columbus, 1968), p. 126. All references are to this edition.

him it is a symbol of Hilda's purity, which he worships. Just the opposite from his Cleopatra, the hand reveals in him a wish to see woman as a saintly being above the level of common humanity. That he should choose the hand as symbol for other-worldliness is ironic, for in the rest of the book the image of the hand appears over and over as a sign of brotherhood between fallible mortals or else as an instrument for committing an act of sin.[4] Yet for Kenyon, quite surely the sculptured hand represents the fragile purity of the dove maiden in her tower.

With Miriam we also encounter contrasting art objects. She has done a series of violent biblical sketches—Jael driving the nail through the temples of Sisera and Judith with the head of Holofernes. They involve the idea of a woman gaining brutal revenge on a man, and they involve scenes, Hawthorne states, "in which woman's hand was crimsoned by the stain." The recurring image of the hand serves to tighten the motif of the use of art objects. Quite the reverse of her biblical sketches, Miriam has also done drawings of domestic and common scenes—such as a wedded pair at the fireside—in a highly idealized manner to stress the charm of an innocent world. In these sketches, however, there always appears a figure separated from the innocent scene, a figure of sadness and isolation. If we interpret the figure to be the artist herself, then these sketches would represent a yearning for innocence in Miriam, who is separated from it by her stain of sin. Probably we can think of both her impulse toward attractive innocence and her impulse toward destructive vengeance as contained in a third art object, her self-portrait. Hawthorne describes the picture in terms of such a duality: "Gazing at this portrait, you saw what Rachael might have been, when Jacob deemed her worth the wooing seven years, and seven more; or perchance she might ripen to be what Judith was, when she vanquished Holofernes with her beauty, and slew him for too much adoring it."

Associated with Donatello, we encounter first the Marble Faun and then the alabaster skull. The comparison with the Faun points up his innocence. The comparison, however, is not altogether flattering. Donatello and the Faun appear innocent in the sense of being without knowledge of moral principle and without the kind of intelligence which morality implies. Both are attractive, but attractive as sensual, subhuman beings. Still, the comparison with a Faun grants Donatello an association with a kind of innocence and with a kind of deification. However, the alabaster skull, reputedly modeled on the skull of an ancestor who had committed a crime, sits before Donatello in his tower

[4]See, e.g., pp. 44, 97, 147, 166, 170, 173, 177, 199, 203, 204, 207, 246, 285, 313, 321, 362, 364, 423, 447, 448, and 461.

as a representation of his crime and of his mortality. In all respects, it contrasts with the image of the Marble Faun. Beyond these two art objects is a third, the bust Kenyon makes of Donatello and leaves only partially finished. This bust does not, like Miriam's self-portrait, hold together the two aspects of his character. Rather, it represents a third stage in his development resulting from the confluence of the two aspects of his character. "It is the Faun," says Hilda, "but advancing towards a state of higher development."

The first art object associated with Hilda is the Virgin's shrine which she tends. It stands at one of the angles of the battlements of the tower she lives in, and it consists of a lamp burning before the Virgin's image. In her "customary white robe," surrounded by the swirls of doves from their tower cote, Hilda is a votary of the purity of the shrine. On the other hand, Hilda is also associated with the portrait of Beatrice Cenci by Guido Reni which she is copying. The portrait involves "an unfathomable depth of sorrow." For Hilda, the sorrow in Beatrice's face results from a sinless fall from innocence. For Miriam, the sadness comes from Beatrice's knowledge that some of the evil of the Cenci family is hers. To both, however, Beatrice is a human being touched by a sense of sin.

In all four cases there is a consistent pattern of contrast. Kenyon's delicate marble hand, Miriam's sketches of familiar scenes, the Marble Faun associated with Donatello, and the Virgin's shrine associated with Hilda all connote purity and innocence. These are balanced against Kenyon's Cleopatra, Miriam's biblical sketches, the alabaster skull owned by Donatello, and Hilda's copy of Beatrice. This pattern of balance in the art objects is only the beginning of contrasts and associations that become labyrinthine before the work ends, as we shall see. But the pattern is fundamental for introducing us to the dreamlike coherence the work has. The characters merge into the art objects they create and own. The result is the reduction of the characters toward the quality of art objects and the raising of the art objects toward the human level. The point where they meet is the level where the romance exists in its world of myth.

The dreamlike texture is complicated by Hawthorne's use of repeated images and scenes, altered slightly each time they appear, but definitely setting up a cyclical rhythm of action that is surreal in its incessant regularity.

An obvious example is the lady at the fountain. She is most fully discussed in the legend from Donatello's ancestral past. The marble nymph on the fountain of Monte Beni is said to represent a water nymph who once lived in the fountain and loved one of Donatello's ancestors.

The lover, however, committed a crime and, in attempting to wash the blood from his hands in the waters of the fountain, caused the nymph to vanish from his life after one final reappearance with his blood staining her brow. Her disappearance signals his break with innocence. But the imagery is more complex than that. "The nymph might have comforted him in sorrow," explains Donatello, "but could not cleanse his conscience of a crime." He implies that the lover sought too much in the nymph by seeking absolution rather than comfort and therefore forfeited all right to solace. This situation is used in transmuted form throughout the book, associated with Miriam. It appears first in the image of the fountain gushing from a naiad's urn in the center of the court where Miriam lives. The effect here is simply a visual foreshadowing of the image pattern. In the next instance we see Miriam kneeling subservient to the model, Antonio, by the fountain on the Pincian Hill, closely resembling a sin-stained fountain nymph. Then, at the Fountain of Trevi, Miriam's shadow is flanked in the water by the shadows of the model and of Donatello. The one portends destruction through guilt, and the other possible safety through regenerative love, the two alternatives open to Donatello's ancestor when he approached the fountain with his blood-soaked hands. Finally, Miriam receives Donatello's pledge of love in front of the fountain at Perugia, and as they depart together Miriam is called "a Nymph of grove or fountain." The image of the lady at the fountain thus recurs over and over, altered each time but also recognizably similar.

The same may be said for the image of the dark or veiled, isolated figure. This image is begun with the legend of Memmius, who haunted the catacomb of St. Calixtus, and immediately it is picked up in the cloaked form of Antonio. Such a figure also appears in the sketches of Miriam, as we have noted. There we inferred the figure was Miriam herself. But whether or not she is the figure in the sketches, she indisputably adopts that role at the book's end when she kneels veiled and alone on the floor of the Pantheon. This scene, in turn, evokes memory of an earlier scene where the spectral form of Antonio was observed doing penance, in isolation, before the black crosses of the Colosseum. And also in the same network of imagery we would have to consider the "figure in the dark robe" who watches Donatello in the wayside retreat on his way to Perugia. It is reasonable to assume again that the isolated character is Miriam, but there is no real need to force such a conclusion. The figure is merely a continuation of the image of isolation that originated in the legend of Memmius.

Another image that appears in several variations throughout the book is the figure with hands out in a gesture of beneficent sympathy.

The most important representation of this image comes in the statue of Pope Julius III, who seems to bless the reunion of Miriam and Donatello taking place beneath him: "There was the majestic figure stretching out the hand of benediction over them, and bending down upon this guilty and repentant pair its visage of grand benignity." But this bronze pontiff is a kind of variation of the statue of Marcus Aurelius on the summit of the Capitoline Hill, which is described in similar terms: "He stretches forth his hand, with an air of grand beneficence and unlimited authority, as if uttering a decree from which no appeal was permissible, but in which the obedient subject would find his highest interests consulted; a command, that was in itself a benediction." Then at her confession scene, Hilda receives a similar blessing from the priest of St. Peter's: "But, as he stretched out his hands, at the same moment, in the act of benediction, Hilda knelt down and received the blessing with as devout a simplicity as any Catholic of them all." Hawthorne repeats and complicates the image when he has Miriam raise her arms in a similar gesture toward Hilda and Kenyon in the Pantheon. Her gesture is both a benediction and a warning to keep back: "she looked towards the pair, and extended her hands with a gesture of benediction. . . . They suffered her to glide out of the portal, however, without a greeting; for those extended hands, even while they blessed, seemed to repel, as if Miriam stood on the other side of a fathomless abyss, and warned them from its verge." As a gesture of repulse, Miriam's movement also repeats Hilda's repellent gesture when Miriam went to her after the murder of the model: "she put forth her hands with an involuntary repellent gesture, so expressive, that Miriam at once felt a great chasm opening itself between them two." Thus, over and over Hawthorne presents the same image in the same language, slightly altered.

The book is framed by two festivals, which are always important to what Hawthorne has to say. As usual, they represent the hurly-burly of life among men. In the first, which takes place at the Villa Borghese during a feast day, Miriam and Donatello dance in a throng of people, re-creating a Golden Age, until the challenging specter of the model appears before them vying with Donatello in the dance. His presence abruptly shatters the mood of carefree innocence Miriam and Donatello had achieved. For Miriam the scene is dreamlike, and, we may be tempted to add, archetypal. "In Miriam's remembrance, the scene had a character of fantasy. It was as if a company of satyrs, fauns, and nymphs, with Pan in the midst of them, had been disporting themselves in these venerable woods, only a moment ago; and now, in another moment, because some profane eye had looked at them too closely, or some intruder had cast a shadow on their mirth, the sylvan pageant had utterly disappeared." The first festival is a microcosm of a fall from innocence. Like a theme in a musical composition, once introduced, the scene recurs fragmentarily throughout the work and finally emerges again in an expanded and much more developed form near the conclusion. In a thematic sense, the final festival scene begins where the first festival ended. Hawthorne describes its beginning as "like a feverish dream." It is both surreal and comic. Kenyon confronts a gigantic female masquerader who shoots him with a cloud of lime dust. He is challenged in a way similar to the way Donatello and Miriam were challenged by the apparition of the model. But the scene progresses and changes. Kenyon is again confronted, but this time by Hilda dressed as a white domino, on the balcony above, who throws a rose to him, in direct contrast to the shot of the gigantic woman. Beginning where the first festival ended—with a confrontation with a frightening challenge in the whirl of human life—the second festival moves to a scene of resolution beyond the challenge. For the moment, however, we are less concerned with the meaning of the festivals than with their texture. Overtly dreamlike, the festivals blend into each other. Characters shift roles. Kenyon replaces Miriam and Donatello as they recede into the background. But the scene itself expands and moves toward a resolution.

This is the sense we have with all of the recurring images we encounter in the work. An image moves toward a resolution or continues to make its presence felt throughout the work, taking clear precedence over concerns of character or plot. These images emerge from the central theme of the work. The psychological principles of association and contrast govern their movements and give them coherence. The resulting texture is that of a dream, where rational principles of organization cede to psychological principles. But more than that, the repetitiousness of the images and their patterns convinces us that we are engaged with a truth that occurs over and over, infinitely. We are convinced, in other words, that we are engaged with an archetypal experience, or experience on the level of myth. That the archetype shifts, Proteus-like, from image to image may bewilder us. But the process of locating it among its various shapes is a necessary one, for it is Hawthorne's equivalent to the suspense of plot and action in a more realistic novel. The excitement generated in *The Marble Faun* is analogous to the excitement generated in much of modern expressive literature, such as T. S. Eliot's *The Waste Land,* and even a modern film such as Robbe-Grillet's *Last Year at Marienbad*. The excitement consists in the reader's effort to pierce through shifting images to the constants beneath their changing surfaces. With these thoughts in mind, we may now look into the book's central theme and pursue the meaning of the work. The method of the book, we will find, is closely related to its meaning.

As several critics have noted, the central theme is the Adamic fall and consequent rise of mortal man. Donatello is the most obvious embodiment of the archetype. His fall and rise form the thematic center of the book. Typically, his fall is foreshadowed before it actually takes place and then re-echoed after its occurrence. It is foreshadowed in the garden of the Villa Borghese when Donatello wishes to kill the model because of the hold Antonio has on Miriam, and it is re-echoed in the legend of Donatello's ancestor who lost the fountain maiden through his crime. The actual fall, however, takes place when Donatello, at the bidding of Miriam, hurls the model from the Tarpeian Rock to his death. Donatello's first response after the crime is to feel drawn to Miriam in the complicity of the act. "So intimate, in those first moments," says Hawthorne, "was the union, that it seemed as if their new sympathy annihilated all other ties, and that they were released from the chain of humanity; a new sphere, a special law, had been created for them alone." The feeling disappears for Donatello when he realizes that the tie consists in guilt for their crime. He loses his innocence, but —precisely like Arthur Dimmesdale—is not able to accept his capacity to sin.

At Monte Beni, Donatello repents his sin and prepares to begin a new relationship with Miriam with the help of Kenyon. When Donatello meets Miriam at Perugia, he can begin a relationship of mutual consolation with her because he has come to accept the capacity to sin as a part of his nature and for that matter as a part of Miriam's. The tie between them now is quite different. It is a tie of mutual support and sympathy, but not the kind of tie that can guarantee an earthly happiness, since it is founded on an understanding of a capacity that both wish to purge from their characters. Kenyon puts it this way:

> your bond is twined with such black threads, that you must never look upon it as identical with the ties that unite other loving souls. It is for mutual support; it is for one another's final good; it is for effort, for sacrifice, but not for earthly happiness! . . . Not, for earthly bliss, therefore, . . . but for mutual elevation and encouragement towards a severe and painful life, you take each other's hands. And if, out of toil, sacrifice, prayer, penitence, and earnest effort towards right things, there comes, at length, a sombre and thoughtful happiness, taste it, and thank Heaven!

From this point on we can consider Donatello renewed. When we see him again, he is prepared to turn himself in to the authorities and submit to social law. More important, Miriam testifies that they have achieved the kind of "sombre and thoughtful happiness" Kenyon had spoken of. One way to see his development is in terms of Thorwaldsen's threefold analogy of the development of a statue which Kenyon expounds: "the Clay-model, the Life; the Plaster-cast, the Death; and the sculptured Marble, the Resurrection." Or we can see Donatello's stages of development paralleled by three art objects; his innocence, the Marble Faun; his agony and education in his remorse, the bust of him that Kenyon makes and revises; and his renewal, the statue of Venus he discovers in the excavation, reassembles, and then leaves as a legacy to Kenyon. As usual, there is a long line of parallels to his movement. By the standards of the realistic novel, Donatello's change is unsuccessful, for much of the burden of detailing his change is borne by images rather than by directly presented action. But in Hawthorne's dreamlike nexus, an image is as dramatically valid as an action.

Miriam and Kenyon find the change in Donatello so striking that both turn their thoughts to the doctrine of the fortunate fall. First, Miriam suggests it to Kenyon, who tells her that she pushes her speculation beyond what she can know. Yet the idea apparently intrigues Kenyon, for later he whimsically suggests the doctrine to Hilda, who rejects it as he did before. The doctrine has seemed vitally important to more than several critics. Yet Hawthorne's reason for introducing it is probably to have it rejected and thereby to set the limits of what can be known about the archetypal situation he treats. Whether Donatello is better for having fallen and having renewed himself than he would have been had he stayed innocent is essentially an unanswerable question. And it is a question that does not need to be answered. For Hawthorne man has fallen; man does have the capacity to sin in his nature; and in treating the human condition as he views it, Hawthorne does not need to go beyond those postulates. Perfectly adequate is the alternative which Miriam says Hilda would give: "that Sin—which Man chose instead of Good—has been so beneficently handled by Omniscience and Omnipotence, that, whereas our dark Enemy sought to destroy us by it, it has really become an instrument most effective in the education of intellect and soul." What most of the characters—Miriam, Hilda, and Kenyon—recognize is that Donatello has advanced out of his debilitating sense of guilt.

Donatello's development contrasts with the development of the model. The model first appears against the background of Memmius, as Donatello did against the background of the Faun, and the model wears clothes of animal skin—a cloak of buffalo hide and breeches of goatskin—so that he looks like an "antique Satyr," an equivalent to the Faun Donatello resembles. As we have already observed, the two rivals mirror each other when they dance at the Villa Borghese and when they flank Miriam by the Fountain of Trevi. Yet more important, their relationships with Miriam are strangely similar up to the point of the final outcomes. From what we can determine of Miriam's past, the model was involved in a crime with Miriam, much as Donatello comes to be. In the confrontation after the festival at the Villa Borghese, Miriam says to the model, "Do you imagine me a murderess? . . . You, at least, have no right to think me so!" He answers, "Yet . . . men have said, that this white hand [Miriam's] had once a crimson stain." And she responds, "It had no stain . . . until you grasped it in your own!" Obliquely, they are talking about a crime that seems to have stained the model, leaving Miriam not legally guilty but somehow implicated. We know that Miriam had earlier broken a betrothal to a marchese of a branch of her paternal house, and we know the marchese had a strange "subtlety" of thin-blooded insanity. It would be reasonable to assume the crime had something to do with protecting Miriam against the marchese. This is suggested by Hawthorne's juxtaposition of the information about the broken betrothal with his reference to the "terrible event" in which Miriam was suspected "of being at least an accomplice." Yet this is only suggested, not pinned down. What we do know surely is that Antonio joined the Capuchins to do penance, just as Donatello was to retire to Monte Beni, and on refinding Miriam, as Donatello was to do, the model recognized a bond between Miriam and himself. Both men, then, enact the fall, but the model perishes whereas Donatello renews himself.

We must not press for too many motivational reasons why their outcomes differ, for Hawthorne is first and foremost using them to illustrate alternative possibilities of the fall. The fact that their outcomes do differ is the important thing for Hawthorne's design. But we may also note two divergences in their developments. First, the process of remorse drives the model insane, while Donatello has the good fortune to be led out of his remorseful isolation by Kenyon. Second, the nature of the bond between the model and Miriam differs drastically from the bond between Donatello and Miriam in terms of control and freedom. The model uses his knowledge of their common sin to subjugate Miriam. But Miriam, in turn, refuses to allow factors of control to enter into her bond with Donatello. She withdraws when she recognizes her presence repels Donatello, and she insists she will not return to him until he wishes her to.

Another alternative possibility of the fall is represented by the developments of Kenyon and Hilda. Both of them try to cling to the idea of Hilda's innocence, despite the knowledge of man's capacity to sin which is forced on them. From the beginning of the work, however, we know they have the latent ability to understand sin. If Hilda had not such a latent ability, she could not have duplicated Guido Reni's process of creating Beatrice Cenci, and Kenyon, without such an ability, could not have created his Cleopatra.

After Hilda has witnessed the murder, she puts off Miriam's attempt to elicit sympathy out of fear of the consequences. She says: "I am a poor, lonely girl, whom God has set here in an evil world, and given her only a white robe, and bid her wear it back to Him, as white as when she put it on. Your powerful magnetism would be too much for me. The pure, white atmosphere, in which I try to discern what things are good and true, would be discoloured." Hilda may have no clear conception of what sin is, as Miriam tells her at the end of this speech, but Hilda's statement shows that she is aware of her capacity to sin. Instead of this knowledge giving her a basis of sympathy for Miriam, it fills her with fear that she will be corrupted and her narrow, moral absolutes overturned. Hence she pulls back into isolation, as Donatello and the model had done. After a time she is able to move out of her isolation toward an affirmation of the human condition. The movement is slow. It begins with her confession to the Catholic priest, an act of communication when she can bear isolation no longer. It continues with her more open relationship with Kenyon that comes after the relief of the confession. He educates her to the complexity of Miriam and Donatello's relationship: "Worthy of Death, but not unworthy of Love!" Gradually she comes to a fuller understanding: "It was not that the deed looked less wicked and terrible, in the retrospect, but she asked herself whether there were not other questions to be considered, aside from that single one of Miriam's guilt or innocence; as for example, whether a close bond of friendship, in which we once voluntarily engage, ought to be severed on account of any unworthiness, which we subsequently detect in our friend. For, in these unions of hearts, (call them marriage, or whatever else,) we take each other for better, for worse." This passage is a complete reversal of the self-interest seen in the above speech Hilda made to Miriam. Having come to this larger understanding of the need to affirm one's ties with other fallible mortals, Hilda is ready to undertake her errand to Miriam's family, an act symbolic of Hilda's affirmation.

Kenyon follows the same course on a much less intense level. He rebuffs Miriam by his manner when she tries to confess her past sin to him. Only after he has been gradually drawn into Donatello's anguish and has his sympathy awakened for his friend is Kenyon ready to hear Miriam's confession. Even then, however, Kenyon keeps a nostalgic longing for innocence alive in himself through continuing to think of Hilda as a symbol of unblemished purity. It gives him comfort and assurance to think of her in terms of such a fixed moral quantity. But after he educates Hilda to the complexity of the crime, she in turn educates him to the complexity in herself. This she does through her act of involvement for Miriam. Certainly the act was more demanding than she thought when she first went to the Cenci palace. Yet when her internment ended, she was satisfied to have served her friend even to the extent of imprisonment. This is the new Hilda that Kenyon may now cease to idolize as a priestess and may marry as a woman.

Thus, at the end of the work we are presented with three alternative possibilities of the fall. The model is destroyed. Donatello and Miriam find a bond of sympathy, but because of the extent that they were involved in the crime, are unable to live together happily as man and wife. Kenyon and Hilda, through their involvement with the crime at a relative distance, survive well. The crime brings them to a broader understanding of the human condition and makes it possible for them to love each other. *The Marble Faun* ends with a balance of alternatives. Hawthorne's way is not to teach answers as much as it is to demonstrate the complex predicament of the procession of life.

The Marble Faun is about the myth of man's fall from innocence. In a way it is the story of Dimmesdale and Hester retold. But retold quite differently. It consists almost entirely of its surface texture. An image blends into another, moves to an opposite, and blends anew into another image. The characters are barely distinguished from the art objects around them; both essentially serve as images carrying meaning. All this may be perplexing to us if we approach *The Marble Faun* with the idea of probing deeply into the psychological motivation of the characters. But that is only one way to approach literature. We would not seek to probe deeply into Eliot's Belladonna in *The Waste Land*. We accept her as a part of the over-all structure of the work and assign her no existence outside the work. We do not ask *why* she is afraid of the sound outside her door; we accept her as a woman who *is* afraid of the sound outside her door and ask how that role fits into the rest of the work's structure. So it is with modern expressionistic novels such as John Hawkes's *Lime Twig*. There again we do not ask why Michael Banks dreams of a phantom horse which will destroy him. We accept him as one who dreams such a dream and ask how his dream orders the structure and meaning of the whole work. So too with Hawthorne. His subject is not four characters. It is the myth of the fall. The characters only play roles in the depiction of that myth.

To suggest *The Marble Faun* exists only on a surface level, of course, is not to suggest the work is superficial. Far from it. The surface of *The Marble Faun* is an extremely intricate and beautifully wrought dream nexus. There are problems with the structure of the work, however. We can divide it into three sections. The first Roman section (Chapters 1–23) mainly concerns Miriam—her sin in the past, her relationship with Donatello, her attempts to confide in Kenyon and Hilda, and the murder. The Monte Beni section (Chapters 24–35) largely deals with Donatello's growing awareness of the human condition. And the second Roman section (Chapters 36–50) centers on the educations of Hilda and Kenyon. The real subject matter comes, then, in Sections II and III, where we see the effects of the crime. However, Section I bulks almost as large as those two sections put together. Hawthorne apparently forgot his success in *The Scarlet Letter* when he began with the fall already an accomplished fact. In *The Marble Faun* he simply takes too long to get to the fall. Then, as we complained at the outset, there are just too many art objects. The device is kept up too long. Yet when we finish registering such complaints, we return inescapably to the fact that *The Marble Faun* is a dazzling piece of experimentation with the shifting surfaces of a mythic dream.

Dan McCall

Hawthorne's "Familiar Kind of Preface"

Nathaniel Hawthorne was never quite sure what to think about his own writing. In "Fragments From The Journal Of A Solitary Man" he confessed in the person of his tubercular young artist, "I have never yet discovered the real secret of my powers." And in spite of his many prefatory essays on what he was trying to do, Hawthorne failed to make a statement that satisfied him; he lived in uneasy contradictions. His son, Julian, once said: "My father was two men." Hawthorne does often present himself as two men, intently scrutinizing each other, each daring the other to cross the line. His "Inmost Me" and his "iron reserve" engage in constant disruptive combat. The conflict was not only in his writing itself—the tension registered as a war between an eighteenth-century style and a nineteenth-century romantic, symbolist's way of seeing the world—but also between the writer and the man. When, after his father's death, Julian got around to reading the novels, he was "unable to comprehend how a man such as I knew my father to be could have written such books. He did not talk in that way, his moods had not seemed to be of that color." And Julian concludes that "the man and the writer were, in Hawthorne's case, as different as a mountain from a cloud."[1] In writing the novels, half of Hawthorne's mind told him that in mellowing the lights and enriching the shadows he was concentrating on essentials; he said to himself that what he lacked in realistic portraiture of details he gained by freeing himself to contemplate the "deeper import" of his subject. But to that idea another part of him said no, and his sympathies remained divided.

As the editor of *The American Magazine of Useful and Entertain-*

[1] "The Salem of Hawthorne," *The Century Magazine*, XXVIII, 6 (May, 1884).

From ELH, *35 (1968), 422–39.* © *Copyright 1968 by The Johns Hopkins Press. Reprinted here by permission of the author and that of The Johns Hopkins Press.*

ing Knowledge he wrote that his job was to "Concoct, concoct." The phrase could be used—as Henry James's warning to himself, "Dramatize, Dramatize!" has been used to describe his method—to sum up how Hawthorne worked. He advised himself "Make all dream-like." And where he succeeded he was able to convey the resonant imagery of dreams, their displacements and symbolic admissions; where he failed he made his work not "dreamlike" but only dreamy: a vague wash of fluttering shapes. Turning his back on the accurate and copious notebooks he wrote to Longfellow that he was plagued by "lack of materials." He complained that he had "nothing but thin air to concoct my stories of, and it is not easy to give a life-like semblance to such shadowy stuff."[2] The complaint is curious since, when he wanted to, he could render marvelously little facts around him and the high points of colonial history. In his prefaces, however, he sets off Actuality and Allegorical Significance, as if a choice were involved between the representation of a thing and the meaning of a thing. Instead of the job of rendering something and relating it to other things Hawthorne often presents his job as a choice between detail and moral. His notebooks betray a mind operating at two extremes: either "An abstraction to be symbolized" or, jotting down a realistically treated incident, "What can I make of it?" He starts from either end, the concept or the image, and then tries to work it out: to find embodiment for his abstraction or a meaning for his symbol. But he seems rarely to have arrived at the two together, seems frantically to be searching for an idea or for a vehicle.

Often unable to find either of them around him, he wrote in several of his famous prefaces that art should inhabit "cloud land." Yet he never quite convinced himself that cloud land was a good place to write from, and in all his definitions of "psychological romance" there is the sense of regret, the sense of something missed. In the person of Aubépine (in the little headnote to "Rappaccini's Daughter") he found himself "too remote, too shadowy, and unsubstantial in his modes of development" so that his "inveterate love of allegory" invested "his plots and characters with the aspect of scenery and people in the clouds," and stole away "the human warmth out of his conceptions." Throughout his commentary on his writing Hawthorne keeps telling us how his stories are "ethereal" and then complaining that they are "cold."

Why, then, was he so determined to write in the way he did and so concerned with defining and re-defining The Romance? Perhaps a cen-

[2]The letter is quoted by Mark Van Doren, *Nathaniel Hawthorne* (U.S.A., 1949), p. 62.

tral reason for his choosing to inhabit his "cloud lands" was that the clouds provided a cover for "the Real Me." In "The Old Manse" he wrote that "so far as I am a man of really individual attributes I veil my face; nor am I, nor have I ever been, one of those supremely hospitable people who serve up their own hearts, delicately fried, with brain sauce, as a tidbit for their beloved public." In his preface to *The Snow Image* he begins by saying that some find him "egotistical, indiscreet, and even impertinent on account of the Prefaces and Introductions," but then goes on to say that they "hide the man, instead of displaying him." *Larvatus prodeo.* In a letter to her mother, in October of 1842, Sophia Hawthorne wrote of her husband that "his vocation is to observe and not to be observed."[3] His friend, Horatio Bridge, said of him that "he shrank habitually from the exhibition of his own secret opinions."[4] And D. H. Lawrence made the classic formula: "our blue-eyed darling Nathaniel knew disagreeable things in his inner soul. He was careful to send out his secrets in disguise."[5] Hawthorne often seems concerned not with getting at "the truth of the human heart" but with softening, even disguising, the truth he saw in that "inward sphere." Romance offered, he said, "a certain latitude."

But, before we investigate more fully what the latitude was and why Hawthorne felt such need of it, it is important to remember that when Hawthorne made his definitions of Romance he was, of course, drawing on a commonplace.[6] In England Sir Walter Scott and Edward Lytton Bulwer elaborated the characteristics of The Romance, distinguishing it from the novel; Scott described Romance as a "fictitious narrative in prose or verse, the interest of which turns upon marvelous and uncommon incidents." For Scott the novel was different from the Romance because the events in a novel were common, not marvelous, and they were portrayed in the context of modern society. In America, Cooper and Simms along with Hawthorne made the most memorable expressions of this distinction. In his preface to the final collection of the Leatherstocking tales, Cooper said that his work "aspired to the elevation of Romance"; he conceived of that genre as somehow better and truer than the novel. Hawthorne often gave voice to much the same

---

[3]Julian Hawthorne quotes the letter in *Nathaniel Hawthorne and His Wife,* 2 vols. (Boston, 1884), I, p. 271.

[4]Quoted in Arlin Turner, *Nathaniel Hawthorne: An Introduction and Interpretation* (New York, 1953), p. 93.

[5]*Studies in Classical American Literature* (New York, 1953), p. 93.

[6]John Caldwell Stubbs discusses the subject in his unpublished doctoral dissertation, "The Theory of The Prose Romance: A Study in the Background of Hawthorne's Literary Theory" (Princeton, 1964).

idea, but he could not go along the whole way and often turns to an irony that takes back the definition in the very act of making it. In the introductory note to *The Blithedale Romance* he complains that America lacks the necessary atmosphere for Romance; the "beings" of the author's imagination

> are compelled to show themselves in the same category as actually living mortals; a necessity that generally renders the paint and pasteboard of their composition but too painfully discernible. With the idea of partially obviating this difficulty (the sense of which has always pressed very heavily upon him), the author has ventured to make free with his old and affectionately remembered home at Brook Farm as being certainly the most romantic episode of his own life,—essentially a day-dream, and yet a fact,—and thus offering an available foothold between fiction and reality.

How serious is this passage? Brook Farm was not altogether "affectionately remembered"—not in his notes, letters, or lawsuit. His early enthusiasm for the project died within a few months; when he wrote the above note on the experiment almost ten years had passed, a decade in which his pessimism about visionary schemes had deepened. How serious, in all Hawthorne's prefaces, are the continuing complaints that the shades are too-retired and that he was only trying to write "a fanciful story, evolving a thoughtful moral?" In the repeated objections and disclaimers he seems at times a bit too satisfied with his limitations. To be sure, there is a good deal of the usual self-conscious and amused dismay of an artist trying to speak about his own work. But in the light of Hawthorne's difficulties and choices one can see much more: often the irony in the prefatory remarks is self-indulgent rather than self-critical, a public pose to avoid the problem he had with adapting himself to the novel form.

But, of course, Hawthorne did not want to be thought of as a novelist; his prefaces, especially that to *The House of the Seven Gables,* are almost shrill in their denial of the novel form—at least the bulky nineteenth century variety, the commodious detailed work of Trollope, Dickens and Balzac, which Hawthorne was thinking of when he distinguished between "the novel" and "the Romance." To be sure, no definition of "the novel" can do justice to a form of such immense possibilities (unless it be that of Randall Jarrell: "A novel is a prose fiction of some length which has something wrong with it"). Henry James noted in "The Art of Fiction" that there is "a comfortable good-humored feeling abroad that a novel is a novel, as a pudding is a

pudding, and that our only business with it could be to swallow it."[7]
James had too much passion for the form, however, to let it go at that.
Later in the essay he writes that

> the air of reality (solidity of specification) seems to me to be the supreme
> virtue of a novel—the merit on which all its other merits . . . helplessly
> and submissively depend. If it be not there they are all as nothing, and if
> these be there, they owe their effect to the success with which the author
> has produced the illusion of life.[8]

No definition of the novel could be more damaging to Hawthorne's
theory and practice of it. That brilliant phrase, "the solidity of specifi-
cation," pinpoints exactly that quality which is missing in Hawthorne's
fiction. For, the very point about "cloud-land" is that it lacks a solidity
to specify.

Hawthorne felt that art should "spiritualize reality." In the forest
scene of *The Scarlet Letter* Pearl sees herself in one of the pools formed
by the little brook. The pool "reflected a perfect image of her little
figure; with all the brilliant picturesqueness of her beauty in its adorn-
ment of flowers and wreathed foliage, but more defined and
spiritualized than reality." It is not unfair to Hawthorne's aesthetic to
say that throughout his life he tended to think that the function of his art
was to work like the little pool. In the person of the pilgrim to "The
Hall of Fantasy" (1843) Hawthorne concludes his visit by insisting that
he is not content to have the world "exist merely in idea"; he wants
"her great round, solid self to endure interminably." But, he quickly
adds, "nevertheless" he "almost desired that the whole of life might be
spent in that visionary scene where the actual world with its hard angles,
should never rub against me and only be viewed through the medium of
picture windows." His final observation is that the Hall is good "for the
sake of spiritualizing the grossness of this actual life."

So, Hawthorne's aim as an artist is based, first of all, on an ideal of
refinement, refinement that seeks a purity in which physical and material things literally fade out of the picture. Yet Hawthorne is oddly
reluctant to stand by that ideal and continually goes back on it in irony,
saying (to quote the most famous example) that if you open a book of
his in strong sunlight it will appear to be only blank pages. And while he
seems at least half-serious, in the person of Aubépine, when he esti-
mates his work as "the faintest possible counterfeit of real life," the

---

[7]"The Art of Fiction," *Partial Portraits* (London, 1888), p. 376.
[8]*Ibid.*, p. 390.

question we are trying to answer is: why did he fail to manufacture a more direct and detailed counterfeit? Part of the reason, surely, is that he did not wish his work to be judged by the laws of everyday probability. In his faltering notes for *The Ancestral Footstep* he wrote that he did "not wish it to be a picture of real life, but a Romance. . . . In the introduction I might disclaim all intention to draw a real picture." That theme, late in his life, appears early and continuously in his writing; throughout his sketch "Main Street" the quarrel between the showman and the critic is: how should the world be seen? "The critic," constantly concerned with "things just as they are," does not tolerate the art of the Romancer. The showman keeps telling the critic to move farther away, to take another point of view. "I ask pardon of the audience," he says.

But, if we look closely, we can see that in the sketch Hawthorne is not just asking pardon of a hostile public; in one sense, the two halves of Hawthorne are talking to each other. Throughout his writing he is a man answering himself. To read his prefaces properly one must be alive to his indecision; there was warfare between his intuition that his books were botched and his attempts to turn their deficiencies into virtues.[9] Although his relation to his art and his relation to his audience are necessarily interdependent, I will separate them momentarily to explore his ideas about the works themselves and then to examine his hopes and fears about the people who would read them.

In "The Custom-House," when he turns his back on the details of contemporary life, Hawthorne cries out "A better book than I shall ever write was there."[10] This statement is absolutely central to Hawthorne's idea of his work. Although the line is endlessly quoted, it has become perhaps too familiar if we are blind to the despair it contains; it is like that sentence so much a part of our sense of Hawthorne, "What we did had a consecration of its own!"—we know it so well we are in danger of being deaf to what the man is saying. Hawthorne believed, in the

[9]In "Hawthorne on the Romance: His Prefaces Related and Examined," *Modern Philology*, LIII (August, 1955), 17–24, Jesse Bier writes that Hawthorne wanted "to explore true reality" and the prefaces define his "aim for superreality." Now Hawthorne did like to think of Romance as aiming at something higher than the novel could reach; what Bier and those critics who have followed his lead fail to reckon with is that Hawthorne liked to think it but was not always able to do so. In his prefaces Hawthorne wavers between his impulse to justify his Romances and his uneasy sense of dissatisfaction with them.

[10]I have treated this longest preface as a whole in an article, "The Design of Hawthorne's 'Custom-House,' " *Nineteenth-Century Fiction* (March, 1967), pp. 349–58.

introduction to his masterpiece, that he had chosen the wrong path. He really believed that "A better book than I shall ever write was there" under his eyes if he could only see it and suffer it into his pen. But he could not do it. What he did do was very great and there was no one else who could have done it. And he did it not by breaking his habit of allegory but by using it in a setting where it could be his best instrument to lay bare the rigid barbarity of the Puritan mind. However, Hawthorne tells us, *"The Scarlet Letter* was not that "better" book he saw in his mind, the book he lacked "the cunning to transcribe."

That word "cunning" is crucial in explaining why the portrayal of "presentness" seemed so hard a task for Hawthorne. In "The Devil in Manuscript" the man responsible for setting the town on fire is a writer; it is the writing that causes the local conflagration. The title of the story is a statement of Hawthorne's attitude: "The Devil in Manuscript" (he was quite literally there, or, as Hawthorne elsewhere complains, in the inkwell). The fire in the story is as demonic as the laugh which concludes it. For Hawthorne, art was associated with insidious force. To quote again from "The Art of Fiction," James writes on this subject that

> "Art" in our Protestant communities, where so many things have got so strangely twisted about, is supposed in certain circles to have some vague injurious effect upon those who make it an important consideration, who let it weigh in the balance. It is assumed to be opposed in some mysterious manner to morality, to amusement, to instruction. When it is embodied in the work of a painter (the sculptor is another affair!) you know what it is; it stands there before you, in the honesty of pink and green and a gilt frame; you can see the worst of it at a glance, and you can be on your guard. But when it is introduced into literature it becomes more insidious—there is danger of its hurting you before you know it.[11]

James can show off splendidly when he wishes to, and he wishes to here; the indictment he makes of the community is a successfully balanced expression of his half-amused and half-outraged distaste for the American idea of art. But James's indictment, so civilized, should not obscure the fact that he himself felt great terror about "the vague injurious effect" art had "upon those who make it an important consideration, who let it weigh in the balance" and the price great art would have to cost him. Hawthorne lies somewhere between James and the stuffy community which James attacks. Hawthorne's deep misgivings about art were similar to James's: writing involved a "certain chilliness,

[11]"The Art of Fiction," p. 381.

a want of earnestness'' which made the writer less than a man, unable to respond with any liveliness or spontaneity to experience—never living, always taking notes. Miles Coverdale and John Marcher are projections of their authors, each character an image of what the man most feared about himself and his craft. But Hawthorne lacked James's brainpower, lacked his integrity and sophistication of emotion: Hawthorne could not devote himself wholly, pay everything, as James did, to the writing. And Hawthorne's frequent retreats into piousness reflect his unsuccessful resistance to the community's assumptions that art is "opposed in some mysterious manner to morality, to amusement, to instruction." He meant it when he wrote to Fields "I wish God had given me the faculty of writing a sunshiny book." In remarking that "my own individual taste is for quite another class of works than those which I myself am able to write," he was telling the truth: much of his writing did appall him.

We may perhaps define now, with greater precision, why it was that Hawthorne was such a determined frequenter of "cloud land." Northrop Frye has written in the *Anatomy of Criticism* of the distinction between Novel and Romance; Frye's account is perhaps closer to explaining Hawthorne's predicament than anything Hawthorne himself said in his prefaces:

> The essential difference between novel and romance lies in the conception of characterization. The romancer does not attempt to create "real people" so much as stylized figures which expand into psychological archetypes. It is in the romance that we find Jung's libido, anima, and shadow reflected in the hero, heroine, and villain respectively. That is why the romance so often radiates a flow of subjective intensity that the novel lacks, and why a suggestion of allegory is constantly creeping in around its fringes.[12]

Hawthorne was working in this realm of "subjective intensity" imperfectly contained and defined by the "suggestion of allegory" on its fringes, a world that sparked with something untamable. It was, in fact, a world which violated his theory of art as prim refinement. He wrote to Sophia that we are shadows until the heart is touched: "that touch creates us—then we begin to be." But he could not tolerate much more than that one touch. There is an intimate connection between his aesthetic ideal of how art should "spiritualize" life and his responses to women. In *Fanshawe* he writes of his heroine, Ellen, that illness produced "not a disadvantageous change in her appearance" for she "was

_____

[12](Princeton, 1957), pp. 304–5.

paler and thinner; her countenance was more intellectual, more spiritual." Slightness of figure, even this faint hint of illness, was Hawthorne's idea of feminine beauty and, as we have seen, it was also his idea of the art of "Romance," something withdrawn from life and "more intellectual, more spiritual." The description of Priscilla's face in the fourth chapter of *Blithedale* is couched in exactly the same terms as Hawthorne's famous description of his tales: "a wan, almost sickly hue, betokening habitual seclusion from the sun and free atmosphere, like a flower-shrub that had done its best to blossom in too scanty light." One of the mysterious moralisms in *Septimius Felton* reads: "Kiss no woman if her lips be red; look not upon her if she be very fair."

Hawthorne shows us his response to a woman who was "very fair," a woman whom he observed at a Lord Mayor's reception-dinner in England. He writes in his notebooks that his "eyes were most drawn to a young lady who sat nearly opposite me, across the table." He then devotes a full page to her beauty: "her hair . . . a wonderful deep, raven black, black as night, black as death; *not* raven black, for that has a shiny gloss, and hers had not; but it was hair never to be painted, nor described—wonderful hair . . . all her features were so fine that sculpture seemed a despicable art beside her. . . ." And while she makes him fly for comparisons to Rachel and Judith and Bathsheba and Eve he concludes:

> I never should have thought of touching her, nor desired to touch her; for, whether owing to distinctness of race, my sense that she was a Jewess, or whatever else, I felt a sort of repugnance, simultaneously with my perception that she was an admirable creature.[13]

The impulse to "cloud land" becomes clearer. Hawthorne's intense evasiveness, perhaps most clearly demonstrated in this passage from his notebooks, enters and controls some of the most complex relationships in his fiction—most usually in somewhat the same form we find it here, a reserved and literary man responding to a richly luxuriant woman: as in Coverdale to Zenobia, Dimmesdale to Hester, Giovanni to Rappaccini's Daughter. And while Hawthorne renders these relationships with extraordinary intensity, he also seems unable to gain complete grasp of his images and events. Sophia wrote to Chorley that "Mr. Hawthorne is driven by his muse, but he does not drive her; and I have known him to be in an inextricable doubt, in the midst of a book or

[13]*English Notebooks,* ed. Randall Stewart (New York, 1941), p. 208.

sketch, as to its probable issue." So much in doubt, in fact, that when Sophia asked him if Beatrice Rappaccini was to be a demon or an angel, Hawthorne replied, according to Julian, "I have no idea."[14] When he gave the original manuscript of *The Scarlet Letter* to Fields, the publisher reports Hawthorne saying, "It is either very good or very bad,—I don't know which."[15] And later he wrote to Fields (April 13, 1854) to say of a new edition of *Mosses:* "Upon my honor, I am not quite sure that I entirely comprehend my own meaning, in some of those blasted allegories." And he could actually write of the childish *Wonder-Book* and *Tanglewood Tales* that "I never did anything else so well as these old baby stories." Hawthorne was often quite out of touch with his own talent, unable to chart its direction or power. He was, I have suggested, a writer who was divided between profound responses to full-bodied sexuality and an intense need to repress those responses, a writer who felt compelled to work, as Frye's definition of The Romance suggests, in a medium where strange and unnatural forces were his subject, but was equally compelled in his prefatory remarks to deny his legitimate province. Unable to maintain clarity about the subversive energies he generates in his Romances he was unable to gauge with sureness his own power as a writer. In his prefaces, at the beginning of a paragraph he will describe as a valid artistic aim what he will denigrate, by the end of the paragraph, as trickery. He seems to grasp that which is legitimate, truly penetrating in his work, while at the same time he tries to dismiss it with a self-conscious smile. What we have tried to see here is the quality of that smile, and what it might conceal.[16]

Part of what explains our interest in Miles Coverdale is that he embodies many of Hawthorne's own misgivings about himself and his art. In the course of *Blithedale,* Coverdale constantly makes veiled comments about the problems of being a writer; on the subject of

[14]*Nathaniel Hawthorne and His Wife,* I. 360.

[15]James T. Fields, *Yesterdays With Authors* (Boston and New York, 1900), p. 50.

[16]For a Freudian account, see Frederick Crews, *The Sins of the Fathers: Hawthorne's Psychological Themes* (New York, 1966). In Chapter IX Crews develops fully his suggestions about Hawthorne's art-theory: Hawthorne felt "some necessary connection between frustrated sexuality and art" (p. 157). Such a suggestion is not very new, but the way in which Crews shows how Hawthorne's troubled sense of his art expresses itself in the tales is admirable and his discussion of "the most curious aspect of Hawthorne's treatment of art . . . that he appears both to mock the impotence of fantasy and to fear its power" (p. 166) is especially interesting. What I have said of Hawthorne's art-theory as it is stated explicitly in the prefaces concurs in main points with what Crews discovers of an art-theory expressed implicitly in the tales themselves.

mesmeric exhibitions, he sounds suspiciously like Hawthorne on The Romance:

> Nowadays in the management of his "subject," "clairvoyant," or "medium," the exhibitor affects the simplicity and openness of scientific experiment; twelve or fifteen years ago, on the contrary, all the arts of mysterious arrangement, of picturesque disposition, and artistically contrasted light and shade, were made available, in order to set the apparent miracle in the strongest attitude of opposition to ordinary facts.

What Coverdale discusses as being characteristic "twelve or fifteen years ago" is couched in exactly those terms Hawthorne used in "Main Street" and "The Custom-House" and elsewhere in his prefaces to talk about his own idea of what fiction should be; in his claim about this art being in the past he reveals his sense that somehow, as indeed history bore him out, the kind of fiction he was writing was coming to a close and the new era of more "simplicity" and "openness" was about to begin. Gothic adaptation, which accounted for the best American fiction up to the 1850's, was now exhausted as a prevailing and viable imaginative mode; that mode was now in its closing years and so were the years of Hawthorne's best work.

In a letter to Fields concerning the sketches on England appearing in *The Atlantic Monthly,* Hawthorne speaks of his "unshakable conviction that all this series of articles is good for nothing; but that is none of my business, provided the public and you are of a different opinion."[17] Hawthorne was never sure about his relationship with his public, how to square his own opinion of his work with theirs. In his early period, when his countrymen ignored him, he did not know whether it was a fact to be lamented or proud of (considering the "damned mob of scribbling women" that they were reading). But when his great critical success came, it led him to counterfeit his real power by bowing to the inadequate standards of reviewers who kept pleading for the edifying moral and happy mixture of "Laughter and Tears." Marius Bewley suggests in *The Eccentric Design* that Hawthorne's real contribution to critical writing in this country comes in his discussion of this problem of his audience: not when Hawthorne is talking about "the relation of the artist to his art, but in terms of his relation to society."[18] Bewley feels that Hawthorne was unable "to reconcile the roles of artist and citizen

[17]Fields quotes the letter, p. 103.
[18]*The Eccentric Design* (New York, 1963), p. 116.

in the context of American society, or to make a workable creative marriage between solitude and society.''[19]

The difficulty began early in Hawthorne's career when he was, as Poe called him, ''the example, *par excellence,* in this country, of the privately-admired and publicly-unappreciated man of genius.'' Hawthorne continued the complaint in the voice of Aubépine: ''He must necessarily find himself without an audience, except here and there an individual or possibly an isolated clique.'' Troubled as he was by the act of writing itself, Hawthorne found his lack of readership at the center of the problem. When did the solitude necessary for work become guilty withdrawal? No one listens. He sits alone. Is the silence out there some proof that the silence in here is the quiet of impotence? He never could get over that; in England he was persistently troubled by the dream that he was still failing, still lagging behind his classmates at school and unable to join, as they did, in the business of the American community. When he took his first breath of real success with *The Scarlet Letter* he could look with some relief back on his early work. He now had a public. But in his preface to the third edition of *Twice-Told Tales* in 1851 he remarks that when the tales were first written he had despaired of being capable of ''addressing the American public, or, indeed, any public at all.''

When he had his audience he was just as deeply in trouble of a different kind. The public, he had learned from bitter personal experience, could hiss and laugh a man down; if he were not careful they would give his writing the same treatment they had given him as a Custom-House official. And when Hawthorne speaks in his own voice—in the stories or in the prefaces—he is not only a writer but also a private man who worries about what people will say of him. That other man intrudes on the action set in motion by the writer; the author of the great passages in the book is not the same Hawthorne who slides in a defensive introductory note. He writes in the preface to *Blithedale* that he does not ''put forward the slightest pretensions to illustrate a theory, or elicit a conclusion, favorable or otherwise, in respect to socialism.'' The book elicits an unmistakable ''otherwise'' conclusion ''in respect to socialism'' but the public man would not admit it.

Often the public-pitched commentary is inappropriate to what his larger self has imagined. The famous preface to *The House of the Seven Gables,* for example, is rather less than accurate about the romance itself. His story, Hawthorne says, will be filtered through a handful of ''legendary mist, which the reader, according to his pleasure, may

[19]*Ibid.,* p. 136.

either disregard or allow it to float almost imperceptibly about the characters and events for the sake of a picturesque effect.'' At the end of his preface Hawthorne asks that ''the book may be read strictly as a Romance, having a great deal more to do with the clouds over-head than with any portion of the actual soil of the County of Essex.'' But he protests too much. In the opening scene of the book this direction to Heavenly territory indicates an evasion. The portrait of Matthew Maule's violent end, ''a death that blasted with strange horror'' his property, does not take place in ''cloud land.'' Hawthorne strikes out at all ''those who take upon themselves to be leaders of the people'' and who are ''fully liable to all the passionate error that has ever characterized the maddest mob.'' Hawthorne's indictment of the Puritans —who massacred ''their own equals, brethren, and wives''—is spelled out in an unqualified passion unusual for Hawthorne's writing in general and surely out of keeping with his prefatory description of his work as ''woven of so humble a texture.'' At the death scene we see ''Clergymen, judges, statesmen—the wisest, calmest, holiest persons of their day—in the inner circle round the gallows, loudest to applaud the work of blood, latest to confess themselves miserably deceived.'' All of this comes only three paragraphs away from the gently ironic preface, at the beginning of the story proper. Hawthorne's preface maintains a condescending attitude toward ''some definite moral purpose'' and wryly indicates that he does not want to be ''deficient in this particular.'' At the beginning of the story itself, however, one feels as if someone who had been repeatedly pushed back into the wings has finally got the stage. There is no butterfly of a story being impaled on the iron rod of a moral; the story itself generates sufficient iron.

Hawthorne adopts, then, a curiously defensive and misleading tone when he addresses himself to the people he hoped would read his books. He continuously reiterates the plea in his famous introduction to *Gables* that he does not want the ''fancy pictures'' of his imagination to be brought into positive contact with the realities of the moment. He attempts to anticipate various criticisms and find answers to them. Uncertain as to what the public might make of his work, he says that he ''has proposed to himself—but with what success, fortunately, it is not for him to judge—to keep undeviatingly within his immunities.''

So concerned was he with keeping ''within his immunities'' that when he attempted to speak to a general public about matters of social concern his voice carried little authority. He hated the institution of slavery, and early in his life went on record against it. But in his *Life of Franklin Pierce* (which appeared the same year as *Blithedale*) he saw slavery as ''one of those evils which divine Providence does not leave to be remedied by human contrivances, but which, in its own good time, by some means impossible to be anticipated . . . it causes to vanish like a dream." Lawrence Hall has said that "it is to Hawthorne's supreme credit that in his appraisal of the political and social upheaval of the war he had the courage to face the facts."[20] This statement is corruptingly wrong. Nowhere is its error more clearly exposed than in the article "Chiefly About War Matters" which appeared in *The Atlantic Monthly* for July, 1862. Here one might hope to see Hawthorne's "courage to face the facts" of the war but what one actually sees is the weakness of his attempt to confront them. "Nobody was ever more justly hanged," he says of John Brown, and "any common-sensible man, looking at the matter unsentimentally, must have felt a certain intellectual satisfaction in seeing him hanged, if it were only in requital of his preposterous miscalculation of possibilities." At the bottom of the page what appears to be a footnote by the editors of *The Atlantic* says: "Can it be a son of old Massachusetts who utters this abominable statement? For shame." Henry James writes that "the editor of the periodical appears to have thought that he must give the antidote with the poison, and the paper is accompanied with several little notes disclaiming all sympathy with the writer's political heresies." James wonders at "the questionable taste of the editorial commentary, with which it is strange that Hawthorne should have allowed his article to be encumbered."[21] Stranger still does the whole matter appear when one discovers that "the questionable taste" was that of Hawthorne himself, for it was he who wrote out the footnote disclaimers; he was compelled to take back at the bottom of the page what he had put on the page itself. He says his article (printed anonymously) is written "By A Peaceable Man." He is, indeed, peaceable—peaceable to the point where he found himself unable to say something and stand by it.

The problem is deeply involved with his sense of his audience, for during these same, last years of his life he could write in a straightforward and courageous way, still capable of setting down his convictions with great force and clarity. He writes to Fields about the dedication to Franklin Pierce which he wanted to be published as a preface to *Our Old Home*. The letter replies to the effort several of his friends had made, through Fields, to keep the letter out of the book. They said that since Northern sentiment was then against the former President, the dedication would hurt the book's sales and Hawthorne's reputation. Hawthorne replies:

[20]*Hawthorne, Critic of Society* (New Haven, 1944), p. 158.
[21]*Hawthorne* (Ithaca, New York, 1963), pp. 138–9.

> I find that it would be a piece of poltroonery in me to withdraw either the dedication or the dedicatory letter. My long and intimate personal relations with Pierce render the dedication altogether proper, especially as regards this book, which would have had no existence without his kindness; and if he is so exceedingly unpopular that his name is enough to sink the volume, there is so much the more need that an old friend should stand by him. I cannot, merely on account of pecuniary profit or literary reputation, go back from what I have deliberately felt and thought it right to do; and if I were to tear out the dedication, I should never look at the volume again without remorse and shame. As for the literary public, it must accept my book precisely as I see fit to give it, or let it alone.
>
> Nevertheless, I have no fancy for making myself a martyr, when it is conscientiously possible to avoid it; and I always measure out my heroism very accurately according to the exigencies of the occasion, and should be the last man in the world to throw away a bit of it needlessly. So I have looked over the concluding paragraph and have amended it in such a way that, while doing what I know to be justice to my friend, it contains not a word that ought to be objectionable to any set of readers. If the public of the North sees fit to ostracize me for this, I can only say that I would gladly sacrifice a thousand or two of dollars rather than retain the good will of such a herd of dolts and mean-spirited scoundrels.[22]

There are no mellowed lights or enriched shadows here. The letter is a perfect example of all that we miss in the prefaces: there is no cautionary, diffuse irony, no cloying playfulness, simply a straightforward exposition of a firm stand. In his letter he has mastered those tensions between his personal sense of duty and his awareness of social demands. But in the prefaces, where he addresses not an old friend but a public at large, he keeps trying to find an escape hatch.

Nothing shows his martyrdom to the problem more clearly than the preface to *The Marble Faun* where he asks of the "congenial reader" he has always written for: "is he extant now?" Hawthorne wonders if he may find his old gentle reader only under "some mossy gravestone." He had before him the example of Melville who had lost his audience and had "pretty much made up his mind to be annihilated." Hawthorne was writing in "a foreign land, and after a long, long absence from my own." Eight years earlier, in the preface to *Gables,* he had been able to make fun of those who vaccinated their stories with a moral; here he defines his purpose as "merely to write a fanciful story, evolving a thoughtful moral." Stendhal dedicated the *Chartreuse de Parme* "to the happy few," that is, to the happy few who would understand him.

[22]Quoted in Fields, pp. 107–8.

Similarly, Hawthorne says that he always introduces his publications with "a familiar kind of preface, addressed nominally to the Public at large, but really to a character with whom he felt entitled to use far greater freedom." Stendhal demands understanding; Hawthorne pleads for leniency. Stendhal was not only a more aggressive man than Hawthorne, he was also far surer of his power: he wanted in his audience those sophisticated and tough-minded few who would have the capacity to realize what he was trying to do. Indeed, in one place he says that not until a century has passed would people have a sufficient grasp of history to sense the importance of what he had had to say. Hawthorne, on the contrary, is thinking not of future promise but of the past sympathy and gentle treatment afforded him by his "one congenial friend." Afraid that he would not find him, "I stand upon ceremony now."

While Hawthorne's prefaces have been widely remarked and anthologized, they are too often taken simply as elaborate definitions of a genre specializing in mellowed light. Their real subject is not aesthetic theory; rather, it is Hawthorne's attempt to borrow a commonplace of literary theory in the mid-nineteenth century, the distinction between Romance and Novel, in order to mitigate his sense of failing his materials and the best in his own talent. We as readers must maintain a double awareness of the fight going on in him and in his writing between what Poe called "the obvious" and "the insinuated."[23] If we do not hear the man's voice, while he makes his little definition, if we do not understand what went into the prefaces, then we cannot claim to understand what they are and why Hawthorne was compelled to write them.

If the prefaces are read carefully and in sequence, they show Hawthorne's growing uncertainty about what he was doing and his gradual loss of power. In the preface to *The Marble Faun* he is obsessed with his own dislocation: the complaint of "lack of materials" is the usual one, but in 1860 it is made with a loss of assurance, a sense that he has almost forgotten why the distinction had to be spelled out when he left "the real world" for his "sort of poetic or fairy precinct." Italy, he says, offers him that precinct; America has "no shadow, no antiquity, no mystery, no picturesque and gloomy wrong." But America *did* have each one of these—the shadow, the antiquity, the mystery, the supremely picturesque and gloomy wrong—when he constructed his masterpiece, *The Scarlet Letter*. The inference is unavoidable: he had not run out of materials; he had run out of a talent to organize them. There is a turn-about from his preface to his greatest work and his preface to his

[23]The reference is to Poe's comment on "The Minister's Black Veil" in his famous review in *Graham's Magazine* for May, 1842.

worst. In "The Custom-House" Hawthorne complains that the story of Hester Prynne is too gloomy; in the preface to *The Marble Faun* he complains that his homeland is too sunshiny. In "The Custom-House" he laments his inability to get down onto the page the details of the world he was living in; a decade later he writes that his latest romance has too much stuffing of local color but, after all, "these things fill the mind everywhere in Italy, and especially in Rome, and cannot easily be kept from flowing out upon the page when one writes freely, and with self-enjoyment." Could Hawthorne say that he wrote *The Scarlet Letter* "freely and with self-enjoyment"? Hawthorne's great gift was the ability to make representative selection; it enabled him, in his best work, to circumscribe the essentials of his subject. But near the end of his writing life he is apologizing for his inability to make the selection, for the elaboration of pictorial effects. What gives that apology its full tragic resonance is not only his admission that he feels his talent has deserted him but also his uncertainty that anyone will listen with sympathy while he makes his declaration. In all his work he held to the notion that isolation was a crime, yet his craft allied him against the community on the side of that crime. In his art and in his life he never was able to resolve the problem.

Hyatt H. Waggoner

Art and Belief

Hawthorne thought of himself as a poet, though he wrote only prose, and as a Christian, though after a Unitarian upbringing he stayed away from all churches, including that one. He found Bunyan's understanding of life truer than Emerson's, but preferred not to commit himself, except in the most general terms, on the degree of historicity in Bunyan's myth. Paradox lies at the center of both Hawthorne's art and his belief.

His natural inclination, both in print and out, was to skirt matters of aesthetic and religious belief, or, when unable to do so, to treat them lightly, with a touch of whimsy or self-directed irony, not because they meant little to him, but just because they were close to his heart. He had a large emotional investment in them, but he had not thought them through in any systematic way and did not believe it profitable to try to do so. The light tone was defensive. He was no philosopher or theologian, and he knew it; but he had to write and live in terms of an assumed aesthetic and an assumed theology, and he knew that, too. He found any situation calling for clear commitment in these matters a little embarrassing.

The relationship between art and belief in Hawthorne's work is, therefore, a subject harder to come to terms with and reduce to clarity than it is in the work of most artists. With Emerson, for example, one comes to his poetry knowing pretty well what his beliefs are. Despite his dictum about a foolish consistency, there is a consistency *here*. The problem becomes more difficult only when we try to square some of Emerson's beliefs with others, or the moods and insights of the private man with the statements of the public philosopher. Or Thoreau: we find the beliefs clearly enough set forth in the Journals, and we may follow the process by which they are worked up into the mythopoetic form of *Walden*. But Hawthorne's Notebooks record, with very few exceptions, either *experiences* which might later prove useful or bare *subjects* for possible stories—a week in Maine with his friend Bridge, a visit to a ruined castle in England, the diary of a coroner, life seen as a procession. They do not normally provide us with statements of general belief. Both Emerson and Thoreau in contrast, sought commitment as strongly as Hawthorne avoided it; and the art of both carries over from their journals a large amount of plain statement of the general truths to which they were firmly committed.

As a writer of fiction, Hawthorne was not free to express his opinions directly, even if he had wanted to. When he spoke out as intrusive author in his concluding morals, in the fashion of the day, he often undercut his generalizations as he was presenting them. When he had one of his characters say he could not separate the symbol from the idea it symbolized, he might have been, and probably was, thinking of himself. As a "thinker," Hawthorne was, from one point of view, indolent, from another, an artist rather than a philosopher: he followed the implications of images, dwelt on paradox, and was content not to resolve certain mysteries. Ambiguity, far from offending him, seemed to him necessary in any fully honest and complete treatment of experience. Irony, the double mood, was the response of both man and artist to most situations.

He went to the heart of the matter once in *Our Old Home,* commenting on his consular duty to advise Americans in trouble:

> For myself, I had never been in the habit of feeling that I could sufficiently comprehend any particular conjunction of circumstances with human character, to justify me in thrusting in my awkward agency among the intricate and unintelligible machinery of Providence. I have always hated to give advice, especially when there is a prospect of its being taken. It is only one-eyed people who love to advise, or have any spontaneous promptitude of action.

Typically, he attributes his failure to understand the "machinery" of Providence to a personal deficiency, at the same time implying that those who think they have a clearer understanding than he are deluded. At this point the lines of his skepticism and those of his romantic heritage cross to produce an almost total lack of confidence in the vision produced by the clear eye of the man of reason.

Since he felt this way about matters of ordinary experience, it is not surprising that he was even more reticent about his religious beliefs than about most matters close to his heart. Untypically. he once recorded the core of his belief in his English Notebooks:

> God himself cannot compensate us for being born for any period short of eternity. All the misery endured here constitutes a claim for another life, and, still more, *all the happiness;* because all true happiness involves something more than the earth owns, and needs something more than a mortal capacity for the enjoyment of it.

But he almost never spoke about religious matters as such even to his family.

Those who knew him best are unanimous in their testimony that he thought of himself, and inspired others to think of him, as a deeply religious man. But on Sunday mornings in England when Sophia and Una went to church, he and Julian would usually go for a walk. When he thought of himself as a Christian, it was in no light or merely honorific sense; and he imbued in his children a lasting religious concern, but they never were able to say later just what he believed. When, after his death, both his daughters became nuns, one Anglican, one Roman Catholic, they were fulfilling what their father might have seen, with no doubt his usual mixed feelings, as a kind of family destiny. Were they, we can imagine his asking himself, the products of their past, fated to move on from where he had left off in his, and New England's, religious history?

He would not have known, for sure, the answer to this question, or at least would not have wanted to say. But the subject might have appealed to him for a romance. If he had written it, we should have had to look in *it* for the evidence of what he thought; and even after we had made due allowance for the dramatic character of the work, interpretation of the evidence would not be simple. For there were several Hawthornes, among them one he tended to be and one he wanted to be. The one he wanted to be often gave assent to the leading ideas of the age, but neither Hawthorne was much interested in—or, as he felt, equipped to deal with—ideas as such, the abstract propositions that engage us as men of reason. This is the burden of his meaning when he defined himself as a writer of "psychological" romance: a probing of the psyche, the secret inner and most real self as it experiences belief in action. Not the idea of man's total depravity as a theological doctrine,

but how one might come to believe it and what the existential consequences would be, this is what really interested him. What would it be like
to be a young Goodman Brown? Not what is the "psychology" of
Brown in any purely naturalistic, reductive, or behavioristic, modern
sense, but what would it be like to *live* a theology? Insofar as a lived
theology is expressible only in the terms Hawthorne chose, the dilemma
of the would-be analyst of the relations of art and belief in Hawthorne is
complete.

In the most revealing statement of his conception of his role as
artist, Hawthorne spoke of himself as one dedicated to "burrowing"
into the "depths"—of the cavern of the heart, we might have expected
him to say, in one of his favorite images; but into the depths of "our
common nature," he actually said. The paradox of the dual, or multiple, Hawthorne is here revealed: "common" brings the *essences* back
into the picture. In general, and for the most part, Hawthorne thought
we could not *know* anything about essence: he concentrated on existence, which he did know, in the most compelling way. But his anti-
rationalism was not complete or his skepticism absolute. The darkness
in which man found himself was almost, but not quite, total. Some
beliefs are warranted and necessary, but not many, and the more precise
they are, the less certain.

The rationalist aspect of Hawthorne produced the works closest to
traditional allegory, complete with their implied systems of moral and
religious belief. Meanwhile the Hawthorne of "the deeper mind" was
creating an existential art concerned not with perfectly controlled but
with haunted minds, not with abstract sin but with personal guilt, not
with ideas but with felt thought, not with things as they are, objectively
considered, in themselves, but things as seen with the mind's eye,
preferably from a distance great enough to blur all but the most significant details.

It is not really surprising, therefore, that the religious significance
of Hawthorne's work and the personally held beliefs of the man himself
have been so variously described. He has been labeled a transcendentalist, a Puritan, an essentially orthodox Christian, a skeptical heir of the
Enlightenment, and a naturalist. With the exception perhaps of the last,
each of these descriptions represents a valid response to some part of the
evidence, to that part that seems to the interpreter, with his special
interest and bias, the crucial part. But bias alone is not sufficient to
account for the variety of the descriptions of Hawthorne's religious
position. Emerson's interpreters presumably have their biases, too, but
no one has ever labeled him religiously orthodox or denied his indi-

vidualism in spiritual matters or questioned his Platonism. Surely, there must be something about Hawthorne and his works which permits, or even encourages, such disagreements.

The description of him as a transcendentalist is ambiguous and, at best, not very helpful. Does it mean he was a transcendentalist in Plato's sense, or in Kant's, or in Emerson's? If it is taken to mean that he believed in a transcendent reality, the description is true but does not distinguish him from most others of his age; but if it means that he shared the outlook of the Concord transcendentalist group, its truth is so partial that it need not detain us for long. To be sure, he created Hester, but he also disapproved of her views. (He created Ethan Brand, too, that notably self-reliant character.) He thought Emerson saintly, but he almost never agreed with his wife in her enthusiasm for the new philosophy. He was "transcendental" in his aesthetic theory, so far as he had thought it out, as "Drowne's Wooden Image" and "The Artist of the Beautiful" will show us, and thought of nature as a symbolic language capable, when responded to imaginatively, of revealing a truth and reality perceived through, but lying beyond, the senses. But such matters as these did not occupy much of his attention: again, as he knew, he was no philosopher, and he thought he had no questions to ask of Emerson as a philosopher. From this distance, we may discern a number of ideas and attitudes they held in common, some of them potentially very important. But for both of them, they were operationally less important than the ideas they distinctly did not share. Both would have been shocked by having their views equated.

The description in naturalistic terms is even more misleading. True, he thought the ways of Providence "unintelligible," but it has often occurred to believers that God moves in a mysterious way His wonders to perform. The term *Providence* signified a reality to Hawthorne, but a reality man could not hope to understand. "I am that I am": Tillich's and Buber's refusal to specify a propositional content for the concept of God has a long history, not simply among existentialists, and, one may well hold, has good reasons behind it. It is essentially the same position as Hawthorne's on Providence. He could differ with his Puritan forebears here without ceasing to be religious, or even biblical, in his thinking. For Job, too, God's ways remained, even at the end, "unintelligible" in any strictly rational sense.

From Hawthorne's own point of view, he was too much the Christian to be a naturalist, even if he did not look, with Cotton Mather, for the signs of Special Providences. If he constantly naturalized and psychologized leading Christian ideas, especially the Fall, it was not because he was interested in denying Christian dogmas but precisely because he was interested in penetrating to their existential truth and thus re-establishing and preserving them. Father Ficke's conclusions in his careful and thorough study of Hawthorne's religion are too well documented to be questioned. *The Light Beyond: Hawthorne's Theology* leaves many problems unsolved, some of them very important to the literary critic, but not this one: Hawthorne was not, in any significant sense of the word, a naturalist.

Much more plausibly, Hawthorne is often, especially in the older literary histories, called a latter-day Puritan. If one comes to this description fresh from those that take the transcendentalist or naturalist tack, it is likely to seem refreshingly apt. It acknowledges his religious concern and differentiates his religious attitudes from those of his more transcendental neighbors. His strong imaginative identification with his region's past, his constant concern with problems of conscience, his relative conservatism in religious matters in an age and region of Unitarian liberalism, his anti-Utopian tendencies in a time of great confidence in progress, his tendency to stress man's finitude and innate sinfulness—all these traits and others seem to justify the old label.

But the more one learns about the man and his work, the less adequate the description comes to seem. For one thing, it almost entirely overlooks the crucial matter of *belief*. Hawthorne was not a Calvinist, and a strict Calvinist might well have denied his right to be called a Christian. Hawthorne, in turn, thought his Puritan forefathers religiously misguided, morally insensitive to the demands of their faith, and personally unattractive. He exposed their bigotry in "The Man of Adamant" and their defective theology in "Young Goodman Brown." Their biblical literalism seemed to him wholly mistaken and the fine-spun arguments of their theological tracts irrelevant. Thanking God that he had not been born in those "stern and gloomy" times, he honored the Puritans for their strength of purpose and moral earnestness and for the seriousness and depth of their grasp of human nature and destiny. He shared many of their concerns and characteristic attitudes without sharing many of their distinguishing beliefs.

His view of the Puritans was essentially that of his age. Despite his close acquaintance with their writings and his imaginative sympathy with them, he judged them, a modern historian would be likely to say, unfairly, betraying a typical nineteenth-century bias. Finding them bigoted, cruel, continuously gloomy, and far too anti-humanistic for his tastes, he condemned them in work after work. With his typical insight, he admitted that "strong traits of their nature have intertwined themselves with mine," but these were precisely those traits in himself that he did not like and tried to replace. He would surely have been greatly displeased to find himself called a Puritan by the scholars. In answer, he would have pointed to his sketch of the Puritans in "Main Street," or to his portrayal of them as among the damned because of their spiritual pride in "The Man of Adamant," or as sinners casting the first stone in the opening pages of *The Scarlet Letter*.

Much more to his liking than the American Puritans were what he called affectionately the "old-time" authors in a more centrally orthodox and less literalistic Christian tradition. His feelings on this matter are at least as important a clue to his religious orientation as is his kinship with his Puritan forefathers. Spenser was his favorite writer —and Spenser was a Christian humanist. Dante was another, and Bunyan, Milton, and Samuel Johnson were others. In those areas of thought and attitude where the American Puritans agreed with such writers, Hawthorne, too, tended to agree. "The Canterbury Pilgrims" might almost have been written by Spenser, and its theme would certainly have been approved by him—though not, probably, by Dante, because of its anti-ascetic aspect. Dante would have understood "Rappaccini's Daughter," and Bunyan might have thought that everything essential in "The Celestial Railroad" came from him. What Hawthorne shared with the Puritans, on the level of belief, was their "orthodoxy," so far as they kept in touch with the central Christian tradition; what he chiefly disapproved in their outlook was their Calvinism and its after-effects, their "heresies," in short.

True to his time and place, Hawthorne thought religion both a private matter and a matter chiefly "of the heart," but insofar as his theological views were formulated and expressed with any clarity, they must be described in terms that will ally them with the traditional, the historic, and, broadly speaking, the orthodox. To press for clarification of these matters, to demand to know, for instance, precisely what ideas Hawthorne held about the Trinity, would result in no increase of understanding: Hawthorne himself resisted clarification in these areas. He held on as best he could to a faith he honored and, as he hoped, shared in its essentials, despite his doubts, a faith he saw everywhere being rejected, fragmented, or diluted—rejected by the transcendentalists, softened and moralized by the Unitarians, transformed into a legalistic code or a simple emotional formula for salvation by the fundamentalistic descendents of the Puritans. To hold on at all often meant reinterpretation of the historical in psychological terms.

From such a religious orientation, Hawthorne wrote "The Celestial Railroad," which shows us his reasons for believing that salvation is not easy or automatic or virtue a matter of simple self-trust. A highly effective defense of Bunyan's moral and religious outlook as against that of the Unitarians and Transcendentalists, it makes it unnecessary for us to wonder why Emerson privately thought Hawthorne's works not worth reading. "Earth's Holocaust" arrives at the same point by a different approach. To those who might reply to "The Celestial Rail-Road" by pointing to the reality of progress, Hawthorne here declares that nothing outward can save a man, nothing less difficult to produce than a change of heart can be really redemptive. Political, scientific, and technological progress *is* real, he concedes, and important, too; but it does not solve the lasting and fundamental problems. Man's basic existential condition remains what it has always been. A creature aware of his guilt and faced with the nothingness of death, he knows anxiety and despair in any society, no matter how "advanced." And though progress does seem to be real in some areas, man may expect many of the old evils of society to return in new forms unless he has a change of heart. Mere political or institutional reforms are never enough: an evil will can find a way to corrupt the best-arranged society. "The heart, the heart,—there was the little yet boundless sphere wherein existed the original wrong of which the crime and misery of this outward world were merely types."

Such a view of evil and its origin may be called romantic, subjective, psychologically oriented, or Christian. All these terms fit Hawthorne and his works, and each of them points to a characteristic which the others also illuminate. That each of the terms has meanings that do not apply to Hawthorne is true but not to the point. Hawthorne is not romantic in the sense of having confidence in the innate goodness of unfallen man; or subjective in the sense of tracing all reality back to the private consciousness; or psychological in the sense of reducing moral questions to the *merely* psychological, that is, to the conditioned; or Christian in a sense that would be approved either by fundamentalists or by churchmen in a Catholic tradition. But his concern with inward, subjective experience and with "irrational man" was the gift to him of the romantic movement; and his understanding of man's moral and spiritual nature, the gift of the Puritans and the great Christian writers he loved so well. Unsatisfactory though they may be, we shall have to be content with such generalizations as these if we hope to clarify the relations of art and belief in Hawthorne.

For he deliberately blurred his eye on some matters, did so as a matter of principle; and for the critic to achieve definitional clarity in areas of belief where Hawthorne resisted clarity would not be helpful. Hawthorne thought truth was to be glimpsed, not grasped, glimpsed under the proper conditions only, not, in any of its aspects that really interested him, to be deduced by cold abstract reasoning or arrived at by any amount of experimentation. Humanly significant truth, he thought, was "of the heart." And it was more given than achieved, given in the epiphanies and revelations of symbols. To the discovery of the kind of truth he was interested in, the wide-awake mind and the clear eye might indeed be obstacles: *his* truth seemed more likely to come to what he called "the passive sensibility" in a state halfway between waking and dreaming than to yield to the purposeful grasp of directed thinking. It was to be found by the responsible imagination, the intuitions, and the heart, in the fullness of personal experience. No wonder he believed he could do his best thinking by following the implications of images. He was right. There is more to be learned about his operative beliefs from even minor sketches like "Fancy's Showbox" or "The Haunted Mind" than from the Notebooks, despite the occasional revealing statements of the latter. Hawthorne's art reflects and expresses his belief; and to a degree greater than with most artists, we can find the belief only in the art.

Hawthorne was an idealist who wrote in the age of philosophical idealism. He did not seriously question the general philosophical assumptions of his age. When he defined the special area occupied by his writing as lying between the real and the ideal—or, when implicitly apologizing for the furry ears of Donatello, between the real and the fantastic—he was using the words in a sense it is easy to misunderstand today. He did not mean between the real and the unreal, but between external and internal, between thing and idea, between meaningless fact and ungrounded meaning. The perennial battle between realism and idealism as philosophical positions is relevant to his meaning. Idealism locates reality in the nature of the knowing mind, realism in the nature of the thing known. One reason why philosophers today often do not feel required to take a stand for one position or the other is that, even if they do not see such problems as insoluble, mere verbal problems, they are inclined to see the dichotomy as a false one, with both camps right and both wrong. Existentially, we cannot separate knower and known so clearly.

It would certainly be essentially misleading to try to make a case for Hawthorne as a philosopher, and I have no intention of doing so. But one of the implications of his work is that he anticipated contemporary philosophy (without thinking the issues through philosophically, needless to say) in refusing the ideal-real choice. Between Emerson, who in his youth, at least, tended to think the world plastic to mind and recommended the theory of the ideal because it fitted our needs and desires, and later realists, who stressed nature's intractable and even alien aspects, Hawthorne took his stand.[1] Fact, he implied, was of no use until interpreted by mind; but mind must always return to fact to keep in touch with reality. Less the idealist (to drop a strictly philosophical sense and turn to a more popular one) than Emerson, he thought he knew some unpleasant facts we must take account of whether we liked them or not. Any theory which ignored them could not be true. But he did not think we were bound to take the apparent meaninglessness of nature at face value: if some dreams were mere figments, others were true.

He invented an art form about half way, at its center, between pure interpretation, or mind triumphant, and uncreative recording, or mind in abdication—between allegory and the naturalistic record. (Both these extremes are mere whipping horses for critics, of course; neither, if pure, would be art at all; neither is, perhaps, even possible, whether we call the result art or not.) Unlike Bunyan, he would not write simply to teach, to convey meanings: he would render scenes, as James would say later. But he would render them clarified, purified of irrelevant detail. He would use facts, but *meaningful* facts, facts taken into heart and mind and seen humanly.

"Night Sketches" begins with mind triumphant in daydream, moves to the shock of the initial confrontation with the impenetrable void of meaningless nature, and ends with the darkness illuminated with the true light, meaninglessness shaped into sufficient meaning by the true dream. In religious terms, Hawthorne seemed to find himself faced

[1]I do not mean to imply here that Emerson's thought is wholly contained within the pat label "philosophic Idealism." Emerson had his experiential side, his pragmatic and even existential emphasis, as the way in which some of his religious thinking anticipates Tillich should remind us. I do not find it easy to decide which is the "essential" Emerson, partly because he modified the early idealism as the years went by, partly because, as I see it, so many of the insights and feelings of the private man failed to get expressed in the public philosophy. In any case, the contrast between the two men that I am here developing is by no means absolute. It is intended to throw into relief certain aspects of Hawthorne's position, not to clarify Emerson's. As I have suggested above in discussing Hawthorne's relation to transcendentalism, Hawthorne was something of an idealist too, as his opposition to materialism suggests.

Nevertheless, after whatever qualifications may be necessary on both sides of the comparison, the two men seem to me quite different, not only in temperament, but in the emotional colorations of their thinking, and so in the final meanings for us of their visions of life. I cannot imagine Hawthorne's ever having written, as Emerson did in the 1836 essay on nature, "Therefore is Nature ever the ally of Religion. . . . The advantage of the ideal theory over the popular faith is this, that it presents the world in precisely that view which is more desirable to the mind."

with a choice between Bunyan's faith and utter meaninglessness, which is what a completely naturalistic outlook would have meant to him. He refused the choice. The true faith, he seems to have thought, would be more like Bunyan's in general outline than like Emerson's, but it would take account of things Bunyan did not know. The faith could, perhaps, be preserved if its form were purified.

For the man, this meant validating the religious vision of his favorite Christian authors by expressing that vision in the language and concepts of a new age, without committing himself to their religious literalism, their confusion of history and myth. For the artist, it meant transforming traditional allegory into a mythopoetic art sometimes close to Bunyan and Spenser, sometimes close to Faulkner, but at its best in an area all its own. For both man and artist, it meant devising a way of distinguishing false lights from true by observing their effects in the night. It meant, ultimately, correcting the dream in order to conserve it. Both as man and as artist, Hawthorne knew how to value the little circle of light in the darkness of human life.

Selected Bibliography

MAJOR WORKS BY HAWTHORNE

Fanshawe: A Tale, 1828.
Twice-Told Tales, first series, 1837; second series, 1842.
Grandfather's Chair, 1841.
Biographical Stories for Children, 1842.
Mosses from an Old Manse, 1846; revised edition, 1854.
The Scarlet Letter, 1850.
The House of the Seven Gables, 1851.
A Wonder-Book for Girls and Boys, 1851.
The Snow-Image, and Other Twice-Told Tales, 1851.
True Stories from History and Biography, 1851.
The Blithedale Romance, 1852.
Life of Franklin Pierce, 1852.
Tanglewood Tales for Girls and Boys, 1853.
The Marble Faun[*Transformation*], 1860.
Our Old Home, 1863.

POSTHUMOUS PUBLICATIONS: NOTEBOOKS, FRAGMENTS, AND LETTERS

Sophia Hawthorne edited abbreviated versions of her husband's journals after his death: *Passages from the American Note-books* (1868), *Passages from the English Note-books* (1870), and *Passages from the French and Italian Note-books* (1872). Randall Stewart's editions of *The American Notebooks* (New Haven: Yale University Press, 1932) and *The English Notebooks* (New York: Modern Language Association of America, 1941) restored many of Mrs. Hawthorne's deletions and corrected numerous bowdlerizations. Family and friends also saw to the publication of the unfinished romances of his last years: *Septimius Felton; or, The Elixir of Life* (1872), *The Dolliver Romance, and Other Pieces* (1876), and *Dr. Grimshawe's Secret* (1883). Hawthorne's letters have not yet been collected, but two gatherings are of importance: *Letters of Hawthorne to William D. Ticknor, 1851-64,* 2 vols. (Newark: Carteret Book Club, 1910) and *Love Letters of Nathaniel Hawthorne, 1839–41 and 1841–63* (Chicago: Society of the Dofobs, 1907).

TEXTS

Until recently *The Complete Works of Nathaniel Hawthorne,* 12 vols. (Riverside Edition, Boston, 1883) has been considered the standard scholarly text. In 1962 The Ohio State University Press began preparing the Centenary Edition of *The Works of Nathaniel Hawthorne,* now regarded as the definitive edition. Eleven volumes—the major romances, the juvenile collections, *The American Notebooks,* and the major collections of short fiction—have already appeared. Forthcoming volumes will include *The English Notebooks,* the posthumous fragments, and miscellaneous writings.

BIBLIOGRAPHIES

Current listings of Hawthorne criticism are found annually in *PMLA* and quarterly in *American Literature.* Also useful are *Articles on American Literature, 1900–1950* (1951) and *1950–1967* (1970), ed. Lewis Leary (Durham: Duke University Press) and Maurice Beebe and Jack Hardin, "Criticism of Nathaniel Hawthorne: A Selected Checklist," *Studies in the Novel,* 2 (Winter 1970), 519–87. For critical bibliographies see *Literary History of the United States,* eds. Robert Spiller et al., (New York: Macmillan, 1948; rev. 4th ed., 1974, with Supplement); Theodore L. Gross, "Nathaniel Hawthorne," in *Hawthorne, Melville, Stephen Crane: A Critical Bibliography,* eds. Gross and Stanley Wertheim (New York: The Free Press, 1970); Walter Blair, "Hawthorne," in *Eight American Authors: Revised Edition,* ed. James Woodress (New York: Norton, 1971); and *American Literary Scholarship: An Annual, 1963–67,* ed. James Woodress, and *1968–,* ed. J. Albert Robbins (Durham: Duke University Press). See also *The Year's Work in English Studies.*

BIOGRAPHICAL AND CRITICAL STUDIES

Abel, Darrel. "Giving Lustre to Gray Shadows: Hawthorne's Potent Art," *American Literature,* 41 (1969), 373–88. A perceptive exploration of Hawthorne's imaginative construction of historical symbols.

Adams, Richard P. "Hawthorne's *Provincial Tales,*" *New England Quarterly,* 30 (1957), 39–57. An analysis of the putative contents and unified structure of an abandoned collection.

Arvin, Newton. *Hawthorne* (Boston: Little, Brown, 1929). A critical biography with astute psychological insights about the nature of Hawthorne's works.

Baym, Nina. "Hawthorne's Women: The Tyranny of Social Myths," *Centennial Review,* 15 (1971), 250–72. The most complete and reliable treatment of feminist themes in Hawthorne's fiction.

Bell, Michael Davitt. *Hawthorne and the Historical Romance of New England* (Princeton: Princeton University Press, 1971). A penetrating study of Hawthorne's use of historical materials common in the popular fiction of his day.

Bell, Millicent. *Hawthorne's View of the Artist* (New York: State University of New York Press, 1962). A thorough analysis of the subject, especially astute in showing how Hawthorne's ideas often differed from the leading Romantic aesthetic theories.

Buitenheis, Peter. "Henry James on Hawthorne," *New England Quarterly,* 32 (1951), 207–25. An informative account of James's shifting assessments of Hawthorne and his work.

Crews, Frederick. *The Sins of the Fathers: Hawthorne's Psychological Themes* (New York: Oxford University Press, 1966). An intense Freudian analysis of Hawthorne's life and works and the most controversial of recent studies.

Crowley, J. Donald. *Hawthorne: The Critical Heritage* (London: Routledge & Kegan Paul, 1970). A collection of nineteenth-century reviews and essays tracing the growth of Hawthorne's reputation and the influence of the critics on the writer.

Davidson, Edward H. *Hawthorne's Last Phase* (New Haven: Yale University Press, 1949). The standard critical study of Hawthorne's unsuccessful efforts to complete four late romances.

Doubleday, Neal Frank. *Hawthorne's Early Tales: A Critical Study* (Durham: Duke University Press, 1972). The only full-length study of Hawthorne's short fiction of the 1830s.

Dryden, Edgar F. "Hawthorne's Castle in the Air: Form and Theme in *The House of the Seven Gables,*" *ELH*, 38 (1971), 294–317. An excellent phenomenological analysis of house symbolism in the romance and Hawthorne's sense of homelessness in life.

Feidelson, Charles, Jr. *Symbolism and American Literature* (Chicago: University of Chicago Press, 1953). A chapter on Hawthorne views his fiction as a profound exploration of the nature of symbolic perception.

Fields, James T. "Hawthorne," in *Yesterdays with Authors* (Boston: J. R. Osgood, 1871). Valuable for its many letters from Hawthorne to Fields.

Fossum, Robert H. *Hawthorne's Inviolable Circle: The Problem of Time* (Deland, Fla.: Everett/Edwards, 1972). A generally stimulating account of the various aspects of time and history Hawthorne sought to treat in his fiction.

Fussell, Edwin. "Hawthorne, James and 'The Common Doom,' " *American Quarterly,* 10 (1958), 438–53. An informative analysis of the parallels between the two writers' major themes about suffering.

James, Henry. *Hawthorne* (London: Macmillan, 1879). An important statement in American literary history, suggestive of the ways in which Hawthorne influenced James.

Kaul, A. N., ed. *Hawthorne: A Collection of Critical Essays* (Englewood Cliffs, N.J.: Prentice-Hall, 1966). An excellent gathering of essays on the four major romances and various central problems in Hawthorne's art.

Lewis, R. W. B. *The American Adam: Innocence, Tragedy, and Tradition in the Nineteenth Century* (Chicago: University of Chicago Press, 1955). A classic treatment of the theme of the fortunate fall in *The Scarlet Letter* and *The Marble Faun*.

Male, Roy R. *Hawthorne's Tragic Vision* (Austin: University of Texas Press, 1957). One of the basic critical studies of the dominant themes and materials in Hawthorne's fiction.

Martin, Terence. *Nathaniel Hawthorne* (New Haven: College and University Press, 1965). A sensitive reading of Hawthorne's works and of the interplay between his personal experience and imaginative expression.

Matthiessen, F. O. *American Renaissance: Art and Expression in the Age of Emerson and Whitman* (New York: Oxford University Press, 1941). The seminal study of Hawthorne's relationship to the intellectual currents of his time.

McPherson, Hugo. *Hawthorne as Myth-Maker* (Toronto: University of Toronto Press, 1969). A perceptive account of Hawthorne's art as an attempt to create at once a coherent personal mythology and a myth for the New World.

Pearce, Roy Harvey. "Hawthorne and the Sense of the Past, or, the Immortality of Major Molineux," *ELH*, 21 (1954), 327–49. An analysis of Hawthorne's finest tale, which defines the major historical themes in his fiction.

————, ed. *Hawthorne Centenary Essays* (Columbus: Ohio State University Press, 1964). A distinguished collection of eighteen essays summarizing modern controversies about Hawthorne's art, its nature and achievement.

Shulman, Robert. "Hawthorne's Quiet Conflict," *Philological Quarterly,* 47 (1968), 216–36. An examination of the severe stresses Hawthorne suffered as a serious artist in a milieu dominated by the American Protestant ethic.

St. Armand, Barton Levi. "Hawthorne's 'Haunted Mind': A Subterranean Drama of the Self," *Criticism,* 13 (1971), 1–25. An intense study of the hypnagogic state of semiconsciousness as central to Hawthorne's creative processes.

Stoehr, Taylor. " 'Young Goodman Brown' and Hawthorne's Theory of Mimesis," *Nineteenth-Century Fiction,* 29 (1969), 393–412. An analysis of the tensions Hawthorne tried to maintain between his symbols and the terms of everyday life.

Turner, Arlin. *Nathaniel Hawthorne: An Introduction and Interpretation* (New York: Barnes and Noble, 1961). A fine assessment of the relationship between Hawthorne's fiction and the texture of his mind.

Waggoner, Hyatt H. *Hawthorne: A Critical Study* (Cambridge: Harvard University Press, 1955; rev. ed., 1963). A basic critical study valuable for its close analysis of patterns of imagery and symbolism.

Winters, Yvor. "Maule's Curse, or Hawthorne and the Problem of Allegory," in *Maule's Curse: Seven Studies in the History of American Obscurantism* (Norfolk, Conn.: New Directions, 1938). A study of Hawthorne as a pure allegorist and an examination of the influence of Puritan theology on his fiction.

Catalog

If you are interested in a list of fine Paperback
books, covering a wide range of subjects
and interests, send your name and address,
requesting your free catalog, to:

McGraw-Hill Paperbacks
1221 Avenue of Americas
New York, N.Y. 10020